Language in u...

UPPER-INTERMEDIATE

Self-Study Workbook
with answer key

ADRIAN DOFF & CHRISTOPHER JONES

CAMBRIDGE
UNIVERSITY PRESS

PUBLISHED BY THE PRESS SYNDICATE OF THE UNIVERSITY OF CAMBRIDGE
The Pitt Building, Trumpington Street, Cambridge CB2 1RP, United Kingdom

CAMBRIDGE UNIVERSITY PRESS
The Edinburgh Building, Cambridge CB2 2RU, United Kingdom
40 West 20th Street, New York, NY 10011–4211, USA
10 Stamford Road, Oakleigh, Melbourne 3166, Australia

First published 1997
Reprinted 1997

Printed in the United Kingdom at the University Press, Cambridge

ISBN 0 521 55549 3   Self-study Workbook with Answer Key
ISBN 0 521 55548 5   Self-study Workbook
ISBN 0 521 55550 7   Classroom Book
ISBN 0 521 55547 7   Teacher's Book
ISBN 0 521 55546 9   Class Cassette Set
ISBN 0 521 55545 0   Self-study Cassette

Contents

To the student

This Workbook contains exercises for you to do on your own.

Each Workbook unit begins with grammar or vocabulary exercises, which give extra practice in the language you have learned in class.

In addition, there are self-study exercises which help you develop particular skills in English. These are:

- Listening skills (in each unit)
- Idioms (in each unit)
- Common verbs (in each Grammar unit)
- Word building (in each Vocabulary unit).

There is also a series of six two-page exercises which help you to develop your study skills. These occur after Units 2, 4, 6, 10, 12 and 14.

After every eight units, there is a Review test.

The Workbook is accompanied by a Self-study Cassette. You will need to use this for the Listening exercises, and for one of the Study Skills activities.

Here is a short description of the exercises in the Workbook, with diagrams showing a typical pattern for the units:

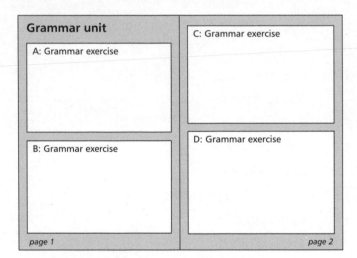

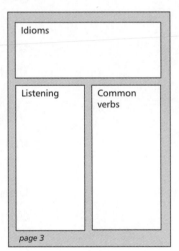

Grammar exercises
These give practice in the main structures of the unit. They usually include an opportunity for free writing, and sometimes a reading task. There are three or four grammar exercises in each unit.

🖭 Listening
These are listening tasks which give you a chance to listen to natural English in your own time. They are usually linked to one of the activities from the Classroom Book.

Idioms*
Each of these exercises introduces around six common idioms, linked by a theme.

Common verbs*
These exercises deal with particular common verbs such as *do*, *make*, *get* and *take*, their range of meanings, and their use in phrasal verbs and idiomatic expressions.

* You are recommended to have a good English–English dictionary to hand while doing these exercises.

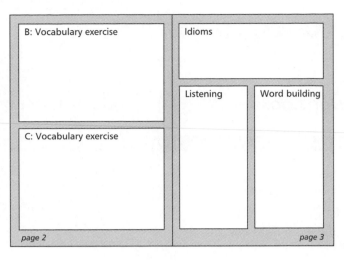

Vocabulary exercises
These give practice in the main vocabulary areas of the unit. They usually include an opportunity for free writing, and sometimes a reading task. There are two or three vocabulary exercises in each unit.

Listening
These are listening tasks which give you a chance to listen to natural English in your own time. They are usually linked to one of the activities from the Classroom Book.

Idioms*
Each of these exercises introduces around six common idioms, linked by a theme.

Word building*
These exercises look at the relationship between verbs, nouns and adjectives, and also deal with prefixes and suffixes.

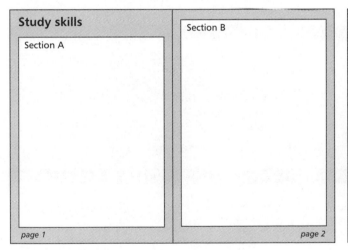

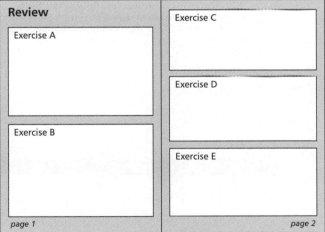

Study Skills exercises
This series of six exercises helps you to develop your learning skills, in such areas as using reference books, reading, dealing with vocabulary, note-taking and writing. Most of the exercises have two sections.

Review tests
These have five sections, and are based on the format of the Cambridge First Certificate Examination *Use of English* paper. There is a Review test after Unit 8, and another after Unit 16.

Guide to units

Self-study Workbook	Classroom Book

1 Present, past and future

Grammar exercises
Idioms: *Common idioms with nouns*
Listening: *Gossip*
Common verbs: *do and make*

Talking about the present; talking about the past; making predictions
Grammar: revision of present, past and future tenses
Writing skills: writing a job application

2 Communicating

Vocabulary exercises
Idioms: *Common idioms with prepositions*
Listening: *Varieties of English*
Word building: *Nouns and verbs (1)*

Vocabulary: types of written and spoken English; personal communication; learning a language
Reading and listening activity: *The truth about lying*

Study skills A

Using reference books
A *Using a dictionary*
B *Finding your way around a book*

Study pages A

Grammar study: *Infinitives*
Language awareness: *Double meanings*
Pronunciation: *Intonation and meaning*

3 Making things clear

Grammar exercises
Idioms: *Colours*
Listening: *Radio news*
Common verbs: *get*

Defining; correcting wrong statements; emphasising
Grammar: defining relative clauses; cleft sentences with 'It ...'; cleft sentences with 'What ...'; participle phrases
Writing skills: Describing a scene

4 Sports and games

Vocabulary exercises
Idioms: *Animals*
Listening: *Cricket*
Word building: *Adjectives and nouns (1)*

Vocabulary: dangerous pastimes; how to play sports and games; issues in spectator sports
Reading and listening activity: *Problems, problems ...*

Study skills B

Dealing with vocabulary
A *Guessing unknown words*
B *Learning new vocabulary*

Study pages B

Grammar study: *Articles*
Language awareness: *Conversational remarks*
Pronunciation: *Where's the stress?*

Self-study Workbook	Classroom Book

Self-study Workbook	Classroom Book
9 Possibilities	
Grammar exercises Idioms: *Streets and roads* Listening: *Return from Berlin* Common verbs: *see*	Discussing alternative possibilities; saying what things depend on; saying how likely things are **Grammar:** will and would; depends (on); indirect questions; probability expressions **Writing skills:** weighing up alternatives
10 Life, the universe and everything	
Vocabulary exercises Idioms: *Things people say* Listening: *Reading the tarot* Word building: *Adjectives and nouns (2)*	**Vocabulary:** branches of science; science and the environment; beliefs **Reading and listening activity:** *Science fiction*
Study skills D	**Study pages D**
Summarising information A *Taking notes* B *Writing a summary*	**Grammar study:** *Time* **Language awareness:** *Conversational fillers* **Pronunciation:** *High key*
11 Evaluating	
Grammar exercises Idioms: *Other people* Listening: *Panel discussion* Common verbs: *take*	Comparing past and present; saying if things are worth doing; talking about advantages and disadvantages **Grammar:** time comparison structures; evaluation structures; causative verbs **Writing skills:** organising information
12 Yourself and others	
Vocabulary exercises Idioms: *Reactions* Listening: *Two jokes* Word building: *Prefixes (2)*	**Vocabulary:** adjectives describing personality; relationships with partners; other relationships **Reading and listening activity:** *Skin deep*
Study skills E	**Study pages E**
Developing a piece of writing A *Jotting down ideas* B *Making a draft and making improvements*	**Grammar study:** *Pronouns and determiners* **Language awareness:** *Regional accents* **Pronunciation:** *Low key*

Self-study Workbook

Classroom Book

13 Right and wrong

Grammar exercises
Idioms: *All in the mind*
Listening: *Mistakes*
Common verbs: *put*

Criticising and justifying past actions; talking about mistakes
Grammar: should(n't) have done / been doing; could/needn't/might have done
Writing skills: balancing an argument

14 Body and mind

Vocabulary exercises
Idioms: *Money*
Listening: *The limits of medicine*
Word building: *Nouns and verbs (3)*

Vocabulary: diseases – symptoms, causes and cures; forms of medical treatment; alternative forms of medicine
Reading and listening activity: *All the perfumes of Arabia*

Study skills F

Study pages F

Reading between the lines
A *Understanding implied meaning*
B *Reading a poem*

Grammar study: *Degree and comparison*
Language awareness: *Formal and informal*
Pronunciation: *Disagreeing politely*

15 Using the passive

Grammar exercises
Idioms: *Sports and games*
Listening: *Oriental spices*
Common verbs: *set*

Choosing between active and passive; reporting using the passive; talking about experiences
Grammar: passive forms; passive reporting verbs; the *have* passive
Writing skills: causes and results

16 World affairs

Vocabulary exercises
Idioms: *All at sea*
Listening: *A minimum wage?*
Word building: *Adjectives and nouns (3)*

Vocabulary: war and peace; politics and politicians; election issues
Reading and listening activity: *On the front line*

Review Units 9–16

1 Present, past and future

A Tenses

Fill the gaps with a suitable form of the verb given. Each of the tenses in the box is used at least once.

GIVE

1 Do you like my old teddy bear? My parents .... *gave* ....
it to me for my fourth birthday.

2 If you ask her nicely, she .... it back to you,
I'm sure.

3 Every time Uncle Jack comes to see us, he ....
us a present.

READ

4 Haven't you finished that book yet? You ....
it for ages.

5 I .... three of his novels already, and I can't
wait to read the next one.

6 There was a power cut last night. It happened while I ....
.... in bed.

DO

7 Last year, kite-flying was out of fashion, but this year everyone .... it.

8 In a few weeks' time, this old car .... 200,000 kilometres.

9 He can't come to the phone now. He .... his keep-fit exercises.

LEAVE

10 It began to get very cold. Unfortunately, we .... our coats at home.

11 You won't see me tomorrow. I .... very early in the morning.

12 My sister's been doing the same job ever since she .... school.

HAVE

13 I love this necklace. I .... it for
nearly 30 years now.

14 Just think – by this time tomorrow we ....
.... lunch in a five-star hotel.

15 Let's go to the pool. I (**NOT**) ....
.... a swim for weeks.

Present simple
I try
Present continuous
I'm trying
Present perfect simple
I've tried
Present perfect continuous
I've been trying
Past simple
I tried
Past continuous
I was trying
Past perfect simple
I'd tried
Future simple
I'll try
Future continuous
I'll be trying
Future perfect
I'll have tried

Two meanings of 'have'

1 to own, possess
This does not have a continuous form:
   He **has** fair hair. (*not* ~~is having~~)

2 to do an activity, e.g. have a bath, have a party, have an argument
This can have a continuous form:
   We're **having** a party next week.
   I **was having** lunch when he arrived.

B Your present, your past and your future

Write two or three sentences in answer to these questions.

1 What are you doing these days? What have you done recently? What have you been doing?

....

....

....

2 Think of a time when you first met someone important in your life. What happened? What was happening at the time?

....

....

....

3 Think of yourself in 20 years' time. What will you be like? What will you be doing? What will you have done?

....

....

....

C Selling yourself

Complete the second sentence so that it has a similar meaning to the first sentence. Include the word in capital letters in your answer.

Example:

I speak French well.
KNOWLEDGE
I have ...... *a good knowledge of* ...... spoken French.

1 I've worked as a tourist guide for three years.
EXPERIENCE
I've .... as a tourist guide.

2 I've travelled a lot.
EXPERIENCED
I'm ....

3 I play the piano well.
GOOD
I'm ....

4 I have qualifications in English teaching.
TEACHER
I'm a ....

5 Working long hours is nothing new to me.
USED TO
I'm .... long hours.

IDIOMS: Common idioms with nouns

What do you think the idioms in italics mean? Choose *a* or *b*.

1 Giving £10 to help famine victims is *a drop in the ocean*.

   a It's too little to make any difference.
   b It's a small amount, but it helps.

2 The entrance exam was *a piece of cake*.

   a It took a long time to answer all the questions.
   b It was extremely easy.

3 The more people get killed in the war, the more they want to fight back. It's *a vicious circle*.

   a Everyone is involved in the violence.
   b It goes round and round without any solution.

4 The people you see sleeping out on the street are just *the tip of the iceberg*.

   a They are exceptional cases.
   b There are many more that you don't see.

5 I paid *a flying visit* to my friends in London.

   a I went there quickly on my way somewhere else.
   b I flew to London to visit them.

6 I'd been working every Saturday, and then he asked me to work over Christmas – that was really *the last straw*.

   a It was the last thing he asked me to do.
   b It was too much to put up with.

If you're not sure of the meaning, look up the idioms in a dictionary.

LISTENING: Gossip

1 **You will hear some people gossiping about these three people.**

   📼 **Listen and find out:**

   a what their names are
   b whether there's any relationship between them
   c what is the most striking thing about each of them.

2 **The speakers use exaggerations in order to be humorous. Pick out the exaggerations which mean:**

   a It's hard to talk to him without being interrupted.
   b You're never quite sure what he's going to wear next.
   c She's always perfectly dressed.
   d She often has her hair done.

3 **Here are some things the speakers say. What are they talking about?**

   a It's such bad manners.
   b Outrageous, isn't it?
   c They're an unlikely pair.
   d Lucky her!

COMMON VERBS: do and make

1 **Both *do* and *make* are used in many common expressions in English.**

   Examples:

   – do your homework, do the shopping, do business with someone
   – make a phone call, make an appointment, make a noise

   Which of these do you *do*, and which do you *make*? Use a dictionary to help you.

.... an effort	.... military service
.... the washing up	.... someone a favour
.... your hair	.... a good impression
.... a mess	.... an excuse
.... a cup of coffee	.... an exercise

2 **Here are some idiomatic expressions with *do* and *make*. Do you know what they mean? If not, use a dictionary to find out.**

   a This coat isn't very warm, but *it'll do*.
   b Have a hot drink. It will *do you good*.
   c It's a pity I failed the exam, but I *did my best*.
   d I feel worn out. I *could do with* a good night's sleep.
   e Why does he want to know? It's *nothing to do with* him.
   f We *couldn't do without* a dishwasher.
   g What time do you *make* it?
   h This room would *make* a good kitchen.
   i I'm not quite sure what to *make of* her.
   j Have you really been in prison or are you just *making it up*?
   k It's too noisy in here. I *can't make out* what he's saying.

2 Communicating

A Communicative phrases

Complete these sentences with an appropriate phrase, using one item from Box A and one item from Box B.

A	B
leave	announcement
make	contract
put up	message
sign	minutes
take	note
	notes
	notice
	speech

Example:

He wasn't in, so I ....*left a note*.............. on the kitchen table.

1 She wasn't in, so I .... on her answering machine.

2 At the conference, the Prime Minister .... attacking United States policy in Central America.

3 It's very difficult to listen to the lecture and .... at the same time, isn't it?

4 I usually .... of the meeting and type them up the next day.

5 I don't think you should .... before you've shown it to your lawyer.

6 Could I have the microphone? I'd like to .... about the arrangements for tomorrow's excursion.

7 I think they should .... in the library saying 'SILENCE: PEOPLE ARE TRYING TO WORK'.

B Small talk

I'm not much good at making small talk.

We weren't on speaking terms for a long time.

After that we lost touch.

I think it's time we made it up.

We've kept in touch ever since.

Read the example, then write a short anecdote (true or imaginary) which incorporates one of the sentences above.

Last week a friend of mine invited me to a party. When I got there I found that I didn't know any of the other guests. I'm not much good at making small talk. I tried talking to a couple of people, but we ran out of things to say. Eventually I noticed a man sitting on his own, so I went over and started talking about the weather. To my surprise, he seemed very interested, and the reason was that he was a meteorologist. Unfortunately, the weather was the only subject he was interested in, and he told me about it for over half an hour. Now I know why he was sitting on his own.

....

....

....

....

....

....

....

....

....

C Language for talking about language

All of the answers in the crossword are words you will find useful when studying a language. You'll know most of them already.

There's no clue for number 9 Down. To find the answer, read the letters in the shaded squares from top to bottom.

Across

2   Learning activity that makes use of a cassette recorder (9)
4   The Present continuous .... (5)
5   *Chair, sugar, dog* and *Amsterdam* are all ....s (4)
6   *The* is the definite .... (7)
7   When we use a short form, like *she's*, we show there's a letter missing by using an .... (10)
11 He speaks with a French .... (6)
13 This sentence ends with an exclamation .... ! (4)
14 This book has eight .... units and eight vocabulary units (7)
15 *Once in a blue moon* is an example of an .... (5)
17 Names start with a .... letter (7)
20 When we make predictions, we're talking about the .... (6)
22 The infinitive is the basic form of the .... (4)
23 Could you .... this poem into Spanish for me? (9)
25 The word *information* has four ....s (8)
27 *In* is a .... So is *at*. (11)
29 'I like reeding.' There's a .... mistake in this sentence (8)
30 *I had done*: this is the .... perfect tense (4)
31 Do I use the Present .... or the Present continuous? (6)

Down

1   *You* and *she* are .... pronouns (they're about people!) (8)
3   The rise and fall of the voice in speaking (10)
6   Opposite of passive (6)
8   *Get up* and *make out* are examples of .... verbs (7)
9   *See instructions*
10 *He does*: this is the third .... singular (6)
12 , (5)
13 *Must, can* and *should* are all .... verbs (5)
16 In the sentence *I live in Rome*, the main .... would normally fall on *Rome* (6)
18 Singular and .... (6)
19 *Slowly* and *easily* are ....s (6)
21 *I have done*: this is the .... perfect tense (7)
24 The study of speech sounds (9)
25 *The greatest* and *the most comfortable* are examples of the .... (11)
26 To make the sounds *m, p* and *b*, you must start with your .... together (4)
28 Speaking, writing, reading and 2 Across are four important .... in English (6)
29 Sentences usually end with a full .... (4)

Now write down three examples of 9 Down verbs: ....

IDIOMS: Common idioms with prepositions

1 Choose the correct word from the box to complete each idiom.

a We're very busy just now, but *at a* .... we could get the car repaired by Friday.

b Of course good quality shoes are more expensive, but *in the long* .... they save you money.

c By the time we arrived, the party was *in full* .... , and the music was deafening.

d *On* .... , I'd say that it would be more useful for you to learn French than Spanish.

e If you're *at a loose* .... on Saturday, why don't you come round and see us?

f So *in a* .... , what you're telling us is that the company's losing money.

g *At first* .... he appeared to be in his twenties, but then I realised he must be much older.

balance
end
swing
pinch
glance
nutshell
run

2 Decide which of these idioms means:

a already started   d briefly   f having nothing to do

b if it's really necessary   e eventually   g after considering everything

c from a first impression

LISTENING: Varieties of English

1 ▭ You will hear four pieces of spoken English. Which of them is:

– a telephone message?
– a series of announcements?
– a speech?
– a lecture?

Where would you expect to hear them? What topic is each person talking about?

2 Without listening again, see how many of these questions you can answer.

a Why are (i) Herbert Neumann (ii) Maria Mancini at the airport?

b What do you have to do if you're travelling to Johannesburg?

c What is Mary Wesley's job?

d Where will Peter's photos appear? Will they all be included?

e What kind of languages are (i) Finnish and Hungarian? (ii) English and Latin?

f What does *seitseman* mean? What is unusual about it?

g How often is the Poetry Symposium held? How long has it been held for?

h Has it been successful?

i Is this the best year so far?

j Does it include: children's poetry? adult poetry? poetry written by local people? foreign poetry?

▭ Now listen again to check your answers.

WORD BUILDING: Nouns and verbs (1)

1 Nouns that are formed from verbs often have the ending *-tion* or *-sion*.

Look at these examples. What verb does each noun come from? Use a dictionary to help you.

A	B	C	D
exaggeration	suggestion	preservation	persuasion
pollution	injection	explanation	permission
promotion	attraction	classification	confusion

What do the items in each group have in common?

2 Change the verbs in brackets into nouns. Which group do they belong to: *A, B, C* or *D*?

a We had a very interesting (DISCUSS) about politics.

b I need to see your passport or some other form of (IDENTIFY).

c She gave me an English (TRANSLATE) of Goethe's *Faust*.

d The Social Democrats won more than 50 seats in the (ELECT).

e They're planning to build an (EXTEND) to the building.

f The (PUBLISH) of her autobiography caused a scandal.

g Suddenly, a huge (EXPLODE) shook the building.

h I wonder what his (REACT) will be when I tell him the news.

A Study skills: Using reference books

Section A: Using a dictionary

Here is part of a page from an English dictionary. Use it to answer the questions.

2 not pronounced: *The word "debt" contains a mute letter* —**~ly** *adv* ——**~ness** *n* [U]

mute² *n* **1** a person who cannot speak **2** *tech* an object which makes a musical instrument give a softer sound when placed against the strings or in the stream of air —see picture at WIND INSTRUMENT

mute³ *v* [T1] to reduce the sound of: *to mute a musical instrument*

mute⁴ *v* [IØ] *tech* (of a bird) to pass waste matter from the body

mut·ed /ˈmjuːt⅓d/ *adj* [Wa5] (of a sound) made softer than is usual

mu·ti·late /ˈmjuːt⅓leɪt/ *v* [Wv5;T1 *often pass.*] **1** **a** to damage by removing a part of: *She was mutilated in the accident and now has only one leg* **b** to destroy the use or form of: *to* MAIM: *Her arm was mutilated in the accident* **2** to spoil: *You've mutilated the story by making such big changes*

mu·ti·la·tion /ˌmjuːt⅓ˈleɪʃən/ *n* **1** [U] the act of mutilating (MUTILATE) **2** [C] the condition resulting from this

mu·ti·neer /ˌmjuːt⅓ˈnɪər, -tən-/ *n* a person who is taking part or has taken part in a MUTINY

mu·ti·nous /ˈmjuːt⅓nəs, -tən-/ *adj* **1** [Wa5] **a** taking part in a MUTINY **b** guilty of MUTINY **2** having or showing a wish to act against someone in power —**~ly** *adv*

mu·ti·ny¹ /ˈmjuːt⅓ni, -təni/ *n* **1** [C;U] (an example of) the act of taking power from the person in charge, esp. from a captain on a ship: *A mutiny has taken place off the coast of South America* **2** [U] a state of feelings or set of actions against someone's power: *He's started his own private mutiny against that teacher, and won't do any work for him*

mutiny² *v* [IØ] to take part in a MUTINY

mutt /mʌt/ *n* [C; you + N] *infml* a fool

mut·ter¹ /ˈmʌtər/ *v* [IØ;T1,5] to speak (usu. angry or complaining words) in a low voice, not easily heard: *He muttered a threat.|She's muttering to herself* —**~er** *n*

mutter² *n* [S] a sound of MUTTERing

mut·ton /ˈmʌtn/ *n* [U] **1** the meat from a sheep —see MEAT (USAGE) **2** as dead as mutton completely dead **3** mutton dressed as lamb an older woman trying to look like a young one

mut·ton·chops /ˌmʌtnˈtʃɒps◄‖ˈmʌtntʃɑps/ also **muttonchop whis·kers** /ˌ··· ˈ··/— *n* [P] a growth of beard on the sides of the cheeks, but not on the chin

force to keep silent; prevent from telling something: *Those who know the truth have been muzzled by those in power*

muzzle-load·er /ˈ·· ˌ··/ *n* a gun which is loaded through the MUZZLE, as in earlier times, instead of at the BREECH (= the back end of the barrel)

muzzle ve·lo·ci·ty /ˈ·· ·ˌ···/ *n* the speed at which a shot leaves a gun when fired

muz·zy /ˈmʌzi/ *adj* [Wa1] **1** not clear: *The television picture's muzzy* **2** not thinking clearly, as because of illness or alcohol —**-zily** *adv* —**-ziness** *n* [U]

my /maɪ/ *determiner* [Wp1] (*poss. form of* I) **1** belonging to me: *my car|my mother* **2** a cry of surprise, pleasure, etc.: *My (my)! What a clever boy you are* **3** my dear polite or humor (a form of address): *My dear sir, I'm so sorry.|Come in, my dear*

my·col·o·gy /maɪˈkɒlədʒi‖-ˈkɑ-/ *n* [U] the study of fungi (FUNGUS)

my·e·li·tis /ˌmaɪəˈlaɪt⅓s/ *n* [U] any form of disease causing swelling and damage to the nerves of the SPINAL CORD

my·nah, myna /ˈmaɪnə/ also **mynah bird** /ˈ·· ·/— *n* any of several types of bird from Asia which are large and dark in colour and can learn to talk —see picture at EXOTIC

my·o·pi·a /maɪˈəʊpɪə/ *n* [U] *fml* inability to see clearly objects which are not close; SHORT-SIGHTEDNESS —**-pic** /maɪˈɒpɪk‖-ˈɑpɪk/ *adj*: (*fig.*) *myopic minds* —**-pically** *adv* [Wa3]

myr·i·ad /ˈmɪrɪəd/ *adj, n, pron* **1** *lit* (of) a great and varied number: *A myriad of thoughts passed through her mind* **2** *old use* 10,000

myrrh /mɜːr/ *n* [U] a sticky substance (GUM) obtained from trees, which has a bitter taste, and is used in making sweet-smelling products such as PERFUME and INCENSE

myr·tle /ˈmɜːtl‖ˈmɜr-/ *n* a small tree with shiny green leaves and sweet-smelling white flowers

my·self /maɪˈself/ *pron* [Wp1] **1** (*refl. form of* I): *I cut myself in the kitchen* **2** (*strong form of* I): *I'll do it myself, if you won't.|Myself a Muslim, I understood what he meant* **3** *infml* (in) my usual state of mind or body (often in the phrs. **be myself, come to myself**): *I feel more myself today* (= not so ill as before) **4** (all) by myself alone, without help: *I carried it all by myself.|I live by myself* —see YOURSELF (USAGE)

mys·te·ri·ous /mɪˈstɪərɪəs/ *adj* **1** not easily understood: *a mysterious explanation* **2** secret: *the mysterious plan which nobody has been told* **3** suggesting

1 Look at the dictionary entry for the word *muzzy*. What do the following mean?

a 'mʌzi
b *adj*
c [U]
d the numbers 1 and 2
e -zily *adv*
f the dot in **muz·zy**

2 Find answers to these questions.

a What is the adjective from *myopia*? What does it mean?
b Does *myriad* mean 10,000 in modern English?
c If you were the captain of a ship, would you want your crew to *mutiny*?

d What would you do with a *muzzle loader*?
e If someone called you a *mutt*, would you be pleased?
f Is *mutter* a noun, a verb, or both?

3 Scan the page (that is, let your eyes move over it), and see how quickly you can find:

a the name of an Asian bird
b the name of a tree
c something that's used to make perfume
d the adjective from the noun *mutiny*
e a disease of the spinal cord.

Section B: Finding your way around a book

Here is the contents page of a guide book to Prague, in the Czech Republic. On what page would you expect to find answers to these questions?

1 Who's the most famous Czech painter?
2 What happened in Prague in 1968?
3 Where can you go swimming in Prague?
4 Is there a youth hostel?
5 Is it safe for women to walk through Prague at night?
6 When's the best time of the year to visit Prague?
7 What currency do they have in the Czech Republic?
8 My hotel is in Hradčany. How do I get there from the railway station?
9 Has anyone written any novels set in Prague?
10 How is this guide different from other guides?

Contents

Time Out Prague Guide **v**

3 Making things clear

A Relative clauses

Here is part of a story in which all the relative clauses have been taken out. Fill the gaps with suitable relative clauses, using information from the box.

> His arms were as thick as my legs.
> It said 'PRIVATE: KEEP OUT'.
> I'd given it to my daughter on her sixth birthday.
> It had my name on it.
> He wants to talk to you.
> She was sitting on reception.
> ~~I'd grown up there.~~
> I'd seen him in the car park.
> It badly needed a coat of paint.
> She wore it day and night.
> I remembered it from my younger days.
> He'd been writing in it.

It all started last summer, when I decided to go back to the village (1) *where I'd grown up* . As soon as I arrived, I realised that it was very different from the place (2) .... The beautiful old pub had been pulled down, and in its place was a modern hotel (3) .... I went inside. The young woman (4) .... was wearing almost enough paint to do the job. I took a room, left my case and decided to go for a walk.

Outside, there was a man standing near my car. As I came out, he quickly put away the notebook (5) .... , said 'Good morning', and disappeared into the hotel.

My old house was a lovely old place with a long curving drive. When I reached it, I saw that the windows were all boarded up. There was a notice on the gate (6) .... Puzzled, I walked up the drive towards the house. The door opened and out came two large dogs followed by a huge man (7) .... 'Can't you read?' he asked. I left.

That evening there was a knock on my hotel room door. It was the man (8) .... He gave me a package (9) .... , and waited in the doorway while I opened it. Inside was a necklace (10) .... and (11) .... 'You recognise it, of course,' he said. 'And now, there's someone downstairs (12) ....'

B Cleft sentences

Rewrite each remark as a cleft sentence. Use the words given.

1 She only needs three hours' sleep a night. That amazes me.

   The thing ....

2 Shakespeare was born in <u>Stratford-upon-Avon</u>, wasn't he?

   It was ...., wasn't it?

3 He smokes all the time. I can't stand that about him.

   What .... the way ....

4 What do I like best about France? The food!

   The thing ....

5 Oedipus didn't marry his sister. He married his mother.

   It .... – it was his mother.

6 They never say thank you. That upsets me.

   What .... the fact that ....

C Descriptive phrases

Here is a later scene from the story in Exercise A. Fill the gaps with an appropriate form of these verbs. Use either the present participle (the *-ing* form) or the past participle (the *-ed* form).

come	hide	pile	spread	swing
hang	lie	sit	stain	tie

I saw a man.
His hair was tied in a pony tail
He was stretched out on the sofa.
He was drinking Coke.

I saw a man with his hair tied in a pony tail stretched out on the sofa drinking Coke.

   As I approached the house, my foot touched something. It was a knife, half (1) .... by the long grass, its blade a rusty brown colour. I hurried towards the house. The front door was open, (2) .... gently in the breeze.

   The room inside was empty apart from a sink, (3) .... high with unwashed dishes, and an old armchair. There was a man (4) .... in the chair, the front of his shirt (5) .... with blood. Whoever had killed him had dropped the knife on his way out. There was a key (6) .... on a chain round his neck. As I went through his pockets, I realised that there was a faint scratching sound (7) .... from the next room. I took the key and used it to unlock the door.

   There was no furniture in the room, just a few old newspapers (8) .... over the dusty floor. (9) .... on the newspapers, her hands and feet (10) .... together with thick rope, was a young girl. 'I knew you'd come, Daddy,' she said.

IDIOMS: Colours

Use a dictionary to help you answer these questions.

1 Sarah has got *green fingers*. Does this mean:
   a she's got no experience of life?
   b she steals things?
   c she's good at gardening?

2 Mario was *caught red-handed*. Does this mean:
   a he was just stealing something?
   b he had blood on his hands?
   c he felt embarrassed?

3 Which would you prefer someone to do:
   a give you *a black eye*?
   b give you *a black look*?
   Why?

4 What should you do with *a red herring*:
   a eat it?
   b take it to the police?
   c ignore it?

5 Your aunt comes to visit you *out of the blue*. Does this mean:
   a from far away?
   b unexpectedly?
   c because she is feeling lonely?

6 Your uncle writes to you *once in a blue moon*. Does this mean:
   a about once a month?
   b on special occasions?
   c very rarely?

LISTENING: Radio news

1 **You will hear four radio news items that go with these newspaper headlines:**

   A COMEDIAN DIES AT 100
   B ANTIQUE TEDDY BEAR MAY BE WORTH £20,000
   C £40 INSTANT FINES FOR NOISY NEIGHBOURS
   D DOG RESCUED FROM WELL AFTER SIX DAYS

   Before you listen, check that you know the meaning of these expressions. Which do you think you will hear in each news item? Mark them *A*, *B*, *C* or *D*.

a legend	an auction
an antiques dealer	fire brigade
an Oscar	a collector's item
confiscate	a standing ovation
commit suicide	a whimper
show business	offenders
sub-zero temperatures	complaints

   🔲 **Now listen and see if you were right.**

2 **Mark these statements true (*T*) or false (*F*). Listen again if necessary.**

   a Burns' 100th birthday show was cancelled.
   b Burns retired in 1979 after winning an Oscar.
   c Burns' death was completely unexpected.
   d The teddy bear is more than 100 years old.
   e The teddy bear can make a noise.
   f Under the new proposals, people playing loud music can have their equipment taken away.
   g Noisy people are sometimes physically attacked by their neighbours.
   h Mr Wright knew the dog was alive because he heard it barking.

COMMON VERBS: get

1 *Get* **is often used in informal English instead of other verbs. Look at these sentences. Which of the verbs in the box has the same meaning as *get*?**

   a Have you *got* my letter yet?
   b Could you *get* a newspaper on your way home?
   c The person next to me on the plane worked for IBM, and we *got* talking about software.
   d Could you say that again? I didn't *get* it.
   e Could you *get* the phone? My hands are wet.
   f The cake's delicious. You should *get* them to give you the recipe.
   g Unfortunately, we didn't actually *get* to meet Prince Charles face to face.
   h I used to think she was rather cold, but she's *got* much friendlier recently.

become	receive	manage	buy
answer	start	understand	ask

2 **Here are six common phrasal verbs with *get*. They are all in the wrong sentences. Which phrasal verb should be in which sentence?**

   a I really should write some letters, but I just can't *get out of* it.
   b No you can't have friends to stay. I hate to think what you'd *get on with* while we're away.
   c They're very upset, but don't worry – they'll *get up to* it.
   d I really don't want to go to the meeting tonight, but I don't see how I can *get over* it.
   e I'm very close to my sister, but I don't *get away with* her husband very well.
   f They haven't paid any taxes for years, and they still haven't been caught. I don't know how they *get down to* it!

4 Sports and games

A Bungee jumping

DRASTIC ELASTIC!

Plummeting to the ground from heights of up to 120 metres attached to a piece of elastic is something thousands of people are doing all over the world.

Already an estimated 50,000 people have tried bungee jumping in the UK alone – and not all of them are crazy!

Some describe it as a close encounter with death; others – the most thrilling experience they've ever had!

So what makes someone bungee jump and what goes through their mind when they're doing it?

'Bungee jumping was something I always wanted to do. I saw it as a way of conquering my fear of heights – and that's exactly what it did,' explains experienced jumper Mark Debenham, aged 32.

'80% of people only ever jump once, to prove something to themselves, but many take it up as a sport and jump regularly.

'Bungee jumping is an amazing experience which leaves your heart racing at up to 170 beats a minute.

'I've done about 50 jumps, both in this country and abroad, and my highest was from 120 metres.

'My first ever jump was extremely frightening. The next seven or eight jumps were still very scary but then after that it was pure excitement.

'When you actually jump you seriously think you're going to die. It doesn't matter how many people you see jump before you, your mind tells you you shouldn't be doing it.

'It takes about four or five seconds before the rope snaps you back up again, giving you a momentary feeling of weightlessness. It's then you realise you've survived the jump and at that point most people let out a yell of relief.

'I've done quite a few different styles of jumping. You can jump forwards, backwards, somersault or jump with someone else.

'People think of bungee jumping

BUNGEE

as being dangerous, but in reality it's extremely safe, and injuries are rare.

'I have a lot of confidence in the equipment and I just enjoy jumping.'

You have to be over 14 years of age. If you're 50 or more you need to have a medical certificate. There are also various other medical conditions which prevent you from doing a jump. A qualified instructor can guide you on these.

It is important that you only jump with a licensed club which is fully insured.

---

1 Here are some questions people might ask about bungee jumping. Find answers to them in the text.

  a Is it dangerous?
  b How many people have done bungee jumping in Britain?
  c Do people do it in many other countries?
  d If people jump once, do they usually try it again?
  e What's the greatest height that most people jump from?
  f How do you feel just before you jump?
  g How do you feel just afterwards?
  h What does it do to you physically?
  i Could my 12-year-old daughter do it?
  j Could my 60-year-old grandfather do it?

2 Using the text, try to guess what these words mean:
  a plummet   *c* scary
  b encounter   *d* yell

B Rules of the game

Here are some rules for different sports and games. Complete each one. Include an item from Box A and an item from Box B in each answer.

A	B
change	cards
collect	dice
give	ends
land	~~goals~~
lose	net
play	player
~~score~~	point
shuffle	square
tackle	trick
throw	trump
touch	yellow card
win	£200

Football

1 The aim of the game is to .... *score goals* ....

2 You aren't allowed to .... if he hasn't got the ball.

3 If you commit a bad foul, the referee might ....

   ....

Monopoly

4 When it's your turn, you .... and move your piece.

5 If you pass *Go*, you ....

6 If you .... marked *Chance*, you take a Chance card.

Tennis

7 If you fail to return an opponent's serve, you ....

8 If your serve .... on the way over, it's called a 'let'.

9 Every two games, the players ....

Bridge (or Whist)

10 You should always .... before you deal.

11 The player who plays the highest card ....

12 If you can't follow suit, you're allowed to .... instead.

C Football hooliganism

What can be done about the problem of football hooliganism? Read the article, then write a short letter to a newspaper giving your point of view.

....

....

....

....

....

....

....

....

....

Chelsea fans riot as team loses in Spain

CHELSEA soccer fans clashed with Spanish riot police last night during their side's 3-0 defeat by Real Zaragoza in the European Cup Winners' Cup.

At least 12 fans and one officer were injured in the disturbances, which began after the London side had conceded the third goal. Fans in the Romareda stadium ripped up seats and threw them at police, who responded with baton charges. There were six arrests.

IDIOMS: Animals

1 Choose the correct animal for each gap (one of them appears twice).

a The manager has brilliant ideas, but he leaves us to *do all the* .... *work*.

b We had to drive *at a* .... *'s pace* through the snow – it took us hours to get home.

c I felt like *a* .... *out of water* at the reception – they just weren't my kind of people.

d I think I'll just have *a* .... *nap*; I'll see you in about an hour.

e As usual, he took *the* .... *'s share* of the credit for the performance, but in fact his wife did most of the work.

f The party's supposed to be a secret, so don't *let the* .... *out of the bag*.

| cat |
| donkey |
| fish |
| lion |
| snail |

2 Decide which of the idioms means:

a a short sleep   *c* very slowly   *e* out of place, uncomfortable
b most of   *d* reveal a secret   *f* boring jobs

LISTENING: Cricket

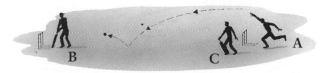 You will hear someone explaining how the game of cricket is played. The recording is in three parts. Listen to each part and answer the questions.

Part 1

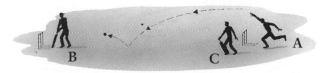

1 What has A just done?
2 What does he hope will happen?
3 What will B try to do? What might B and C do?

Part 2

1 What will happen if:
   a D catches the ball before it hits the ground?
   b B and C manage to run to the other wicket?
   c the ball goes right out of the field?

2 Complete these sentences.
   a You're *bowled out* if the bowler manages to …
   b You're also *out* if you put your leg …
   c You're *run out* if one of the other side can … while you're running.
   d When all the batsmen in one team are out, …

Part 3

1 How long does an international cricket match last?
2 How long does a World Cup match last?

WORD BUILDING: Adjectives and nouns (1)

1 Adjectives that come from nouns often have one of these endings:

| -able | -al | -ous | -ful | -y |

Look at these examples. What noun does each adjective come from?

A	*B*	*C*
comfortable	industrial	famous
miserable	grammatical	religious

D	*E*
harmful	muddy
useful	angry

2 Which nouns in the sentences below need to be changed into adjectives? Change them into the correct form, using a dictionary to help you.

a I love this room – it's so light and space.
b He's not a very adventure person – he's never been abroad in his life.
c I'm afraid my attempts to speak French weren't very success.
d Be care how you drive. The roads are very ice.
e Their marriage was so disaster that they decided to get divorced immediately.
f They say that Liberty's is the most fashion café in town at the moment.

B Study skills: Dealing with vocabulary

Section A: Guessing unknown words

It is often possible to guess the meaning of unfamiliar words when you come across them in reading. Try this experiment:

1 Read Part 1 of the text about the Gobi Desert in central Asia. Do not look up any words in a dictionary, but write down all the words that are new to you.

2 Try to guess the meaning of the words (write them in your own language, or write what they mean in English).

3 Now check the meanings in a dictionary. How many of the words did you really need to look up?

Think just about the words you couldn't guess. How many did you really need to know in order to understand the text?

Section B: Learning new vocabulary

When we read, we often come across words or phrases that seem worth noting down and remembering. It is useful to learn not just the word on its own, but other words or phrases that go with it. For example, here are words and expressions that naturally come before and after the verb *extend* (line 4).

The mountains The land	*extended*	for miles. in every direction. as far as the eye could see.

1 Look at these notes. Which word from the text is missing from each one?

a deeply / seriously } —— { hills / slopes / coastline

d the —— of { the wind / mourners (at funeral) / babies

b —— { snow / job / address

e to —— { a contrast / a problem / a difficulty

c to —— someone { into danger / to his/her death

2 Read Part 2 of the text. Using a dictionary to help you, note down a few useful words together with other words or expressions that naturally go with them.

Part 1   Beyond the camel-herders' tent was a wonderful contrast. For another four miles the Gobi continued flat, then came a mountain wall. There were no real foothills, just a few deeply eroded slopes before the bare rock began. Then the land reared steeply upward across a front that extended as far as the eye could see in either direction. It was the northern face of the Gobi Altai Mountains, a small sector of a rampart 1000 miles long. On the far side lay China. Standing on shifting sand among noisy camels, it seemed odd to look up and see on the main crest of the nearest ridge a white line – permanent snow. As if to accentuate the contrasts, a line of eight crescent sand-dunes lay against the foot of the rock wall. They were glowing butter yellow in the evening sunlight. Hundreds of similar dunes would merge further south-east to form a sand-sea with ridges 250 feet high. When the gale sweeps across these sandhills, the sands shift and moan with musical notes. Early writers believed the sound to be the wailing of demons trying to lure caravan travellers to their deaths.

Part 2   As if that combination of mountain, desert and snow were not arresting enough, I could see a lake shimmering beside the dunes. But it was a mirage. The light was reflecting off a white expanse of salty mud, dried as hard as cement and cracked into crazy paving with a web of fissures. Thirty-five years earlier there had indeed been a lake here, with fish and gulls and reed-beds. After the rainy season it spread outwards for ten miles from the foot of the mountains. Then came an earthquake. The local inhabitants said that the earth's crust must have split because the water drained away downwards, leaving the fish to die in a desert.

5 Set in the past

A Previous actions and activities

Complete these paragraphs with flashbacks using the Past perfect simple and the Past perfect continuous.

Example:

He explained how the accident had happened. Apparently, *he'd been driving home when a young girl had run out into the road in front of him. He'd swerved to avoid her, and had crashed into a parked car.*

1 I suddenly remembered where I'd seen her before. ....

....

....

....

2 When they got home, they were both soaking wet. Apparently, ...

....

....

....

3 After her first day working as a waitress, she was absolutely exhausted. ....

....

....

....

B Reporting verbs

1 Which of the verbs in the box fit into these sentences? In most cases there is more than one answer.

accused	denied	promised	reminded	warned
admitted	offered	refused	threatened	

a He .... stealing the money.   ....

b They .... that they'd been there.   ....

c She .... him of stealing the money.   ....

d I .... them not to drink the tap water. ....

e He .... to give us a lift home.   ....

f They .... to smash my camera.   ....

2 Now choose three of the verbs that go together well (e.g. *accuse – deny – admit*, *warn – refuse – threaten*) and write a short anecdote that includes all three.

....

....

....

....

....

....

C Relative clauses

Improve these paragraphs by using relative clauses where appropriate.

1 Sir Arthur Conan Doyle worked as a doctor before he turned to writing. Conan Doyle's Sherlock Holmes stories are known all over the world. Holmes lived at 221B Baker Street in London. Holmes was an opium addict and a violinist as well as a brilliant detective. There is now a Sherlock Holmes museum at 221B Baker Street. Holmes's friend Doctor Watson was probably based on Conan Doyle himself. Doctor Watson narrates the stories. The best known Sherlock Holmes story is probably *The Hound of the Baskervilles*. Conan Doyle wrote *The Hound of the Baskervilles* in 1902.

Sir Arthur Conan Doyle, whose Sherlock Holmes stories are known all over the world, worked as a doctor before he

turned to writing. Holmes, who

....

....

....

....

....

2 According to legend, the famous labyrinth in Crete was built by Daedalus. The Minotaur was imprisoned in the labyrinth. Daedalus was a master craftsman from Athens. Afterwards, Daedalus was not allowed to leave. Daedalus's son Icarus had come with him. So they decided to escape using two enormous pairs of wings. Daedalus had made the wings out of feathers. Unfortunately Icarus ignored his father's warning about not flying too close to the sun. Icarus was a typical teenager. The sun melted the wax and Icarus fell to his death. The feathers had been attached to the wings with wax.

According to legend, the famous labyrinth in Crete, in which the Minotaur was imprisoned, was built by Daedalus,

....

....

....

....

....

....

IDIOMS: Numbers

Look at these sentences. See if you can guess from the context what the idioms in italics mean.

1 I applied for five jobs, and I had three interviews, but I didn't get anything. So now I'm *back to square one*.

....

2 I'm *in two minds about* playing football tomorrow. It'd be good to get some exercise, but I've just got so many other things to do.

....

3 English courses are *two a penny* these days – you certainly won't have any trouble getting into one.

....

4 I wondered why Paolo and Marina always seemed to go out at the same time. Then I *put two and two together* and realised she was his girlfriend.

5 Then I got a letter out of the blue telling me I'd been given the sack. It absolutely *knocked me for six*.

....

6 Things went from bad to worse, but *at the eleventh hour* the government intervened and rescued the company from bankruptcy.

....

Use a dictionary to check your answers.

LISTENING: Holiday incident

1 🔲 You will hear a woman describing something that happened while she was on holiday. The recording is in three parts. Listen to each part and answer the questions.

Part 1

a Who was the woman with and what were they doing?
b What is the RAC? Were they members?
c Was the woman an experienced driver?
d What was the road like?

Part 2

What does the woman say about:

a concrete posts?
b a river?
c music?

Part 3

Are these statements true or false?

a The car was slightly damaged.
b The people in the village were very helpful.
c It took them a long time to get home.
d It cost them a lot to get home.
e They annoyed their neighbours.

2 🔲 Listen to Part 1 again, and find:
a four relative clauses
b three 'flashbacks' using the Past perfect tense.

COMMON VERBS: go

1 Apart from its basic meaning (e.g. *He went home*), *go* is also used in many other ways in English.

Match the use of *go* in these sentences with the paraphrases in the box.

a My money's *gone*!
b This path *goes* to the village.
c Most of her money *goes* on expensive clothes.
d One – two – three – *go*!
e The cat *went* 'Miaow' and jumped on my lap.
f I'm afraid the bread has *gone* a bit stale.
g The milk can *go* in the fridge.
h This towel won't *go* in the suitcase.
i I can't get the car to *go*.
j My voice has *gone*.
k The party *went* well.
l How does that tune *go*?

I can't speak.	It was a success.
It's disappeared.	It won't start.
It's not fresh.	It leads there.
There's no room for it.	Put it there.
Start running.	I can't remember it.
It's the noise it made.	It's how she spends it.

2 Here are some idiomatic expressions with *go*. Do you know what they mean? If not, use a dictionary to find out.

a His business has *gone bankrupt*.
b He's *on the go* nearly all the time.
c Why don't you *let yourself go* and have a good time?
d Do you think this tie *goes with* my jacket?
e I see petrol has *gone up* again.

6 Do it yourself

A Getting the picture

1 The missing elements from these camera instructions are listed in the box below. Where does each element belong?

---

1 Inserting batteries

Open the cover of the battery compartment (10).
Insert two alkali batteries (AA), ensuring they are
positioned correctly.
Note:
-
-

2 Turning the camera on

To turn the camera on, open the lens cover (8).

3 Loading the camera
- Open the back of the camera (11).
-
-
-
-

4 Automatic wind

After each photo, the film is wound on
automatically. The counter window (1)
displays the current number.

5 Taking a photo
- Open the lens cover.
- Set the flash selector (6) to 'Auto Flash'.
-
-
-
-
-

6 Rewinding the film
-
-
-
-

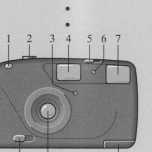
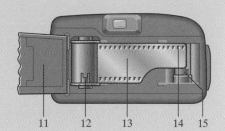

---

2 **Find words and phrases in the instructions which mean:**

a a long time

....

b not enough

....

c make sure

....

d put in

....

e shows

....

f in the right place

....

g hidden

....

h take out

....

A Ensure that the lens is not obscured by your finger or hair.

B Open the back of the camera and remove the film.

C Press the shutter button. (If there is insufficient light, the flash will operate automatically.)

D The film will rewind and the counter will reverse until it reaches 'S'.

E With the back still open, press the shutter button to check that the film winds on correctly.

F When the film is rewound, it will stop automatically.

G Pull out the film until it lies over the drum on the right (15). Ensure that the holes fit over the sprockets (14).

H Press the rewind button.

I Wait until the light (4) comes on, indicating that the camera is ready to take a photo.

J The film will automatically wind on to the next picture.

K To extend battery life, remove batteries if the camera is not in use for an extended period.

L If you are not going to take another photo immediately, close the lens cover.

M Always replace both batteries together.

N Insert the film spool in the holder on the left (12).

O Close the back of the camera and press the shutter button repeatedly until the number '1' appears in the counter window (1).

B Things need doing

Fill each gap with an appropriate form of a word from the box.

1 My shirt's got a coffee .... on it, and there are two buttons ....
   They need .... on again.

2 This kitchen needs .... The paint's .... off the wall, and there are
   .... in the plaster.

3 Look at this .... patch on the floor. I think there must be a .... in
   one of the pipes. It ought to be ....

4 The wood in this window frame is all .... The whole thing will have to be
   ....

crack
damp
leak
missing
peel
redecorate
repair
replace
rotten
sew
stain

**Now think of some similar jobs that you need to do. What's wrong? And what needs doing?
Write a few sentences.**

....

....

....

....

....

....

C Verbs in the kitchen

**All the answers are things you do when cooking a meal. Read the definitions, and write the
answers in the diagram.**

 1 Boil (e.g. a sauce) gently (6)
 2 Cook (e.g. bread) in the oven (4)
 3 Move (e.g. a sauce) round and round with a spoon (4)
 4 Heat (e.g. butter) so that it becomes liquid (4)
 5 Remove the skin from (e.g. an onion, an orange) (4)
 6 Drop a light covering of (e.g. salt, herbs) over (e.g. a pan of food) (8)
 7 Cut (e.g. a tomato) into thin wide flat pieces (5)
 8 Cut (e.g. an onion) into small pieces (4)
 9 Put food on the table for people to eat (5)
10 Cook (e.g. a piece of steak) in hot oil (3)

**Now look in the shaded squares. If your answers are correct, you'll find
someone for whom all these things are very easy.**

IDIOMS: Parts of the body (1)

brain
eyes
fingers
leg
head
heels

1 **Choose the correct word for each gap (one of them appears three times).**

a I can't give you an exact figure *off the top of my* ......*head*......, but I think we employ about 100 people.

b She seems to *have* clothes *on the* .... – she can't talk about anything else.

c He's ......*head*...... *over* ......*hill*...... in love with her.

d I can't take any time off now – I'm *up to my* ......*eyes*...... in work.

e Have you really won the lottery or are you just *pulling my* ......*leg*......?

f I hope you do well in the driving test – I'll *keep my* ......*fingers*...... *crossed* for you.

g I went to a lecture on Chaos Theory, but I'm afraid it was all rather *above my* ....

2 **Decide which of these idioms means:**

a be very busy with something   c too hard to understand   e spontaneously   g tell a lie as a joke
b be obsessed by something   d wish someone good luck   f totally

LISTENING: How to do it

1 **You will hear people demonstrating how to:**

A paint a door
B play the recorder
C mend a bicycle puncture.

Before you listen, decide which of these words you expect to hear in each description. Write *A*, *B* or *C*. (Some words may appear in more than one description.)

sandpaper	brush	hole	stir
thumb	can	stick	blow
finger	glue	drip	

🔲 **Now listen and see if you were right.**

2 🔲 **Use the recordings to help you complete these notes.**

A .... the paint until it's ....

together. .... the .... against the

side of the .... until the paint stops

.... the paint on, moving the

.... smoothly up and down.

B .... the recorder in both hands.

.... the .... underneath with your

left .... Put your right .... over

the first .... , and .... gently.

C .... round the .... with ....

Spread the .... round with your ....

.... the back off the patch and................

it firmly over the .... Then leave it to

....

WORD BUILDING: Prefixes (1)

un-	in-	im-	ir-	il-

1 **These prefixes have the meaning *not* or *the opposite of*. Look at these examples:**

*un*likely   *im*possible   *il*logical
*in*efficient   *ir*regular

2 **Use a dictionary to find the opposites of these words, and write the prefixes.**

..............comfortable   ....fortunate
..............legible   ....practical
..............edible   ....literate
..............expected   ....audible
..............patient   ....relevant

3 **Replace the expressions in italics with words from Section 2.**

a Ugh! This meat is *impossible to eat*.
b He spoke so quietly that his voice was almost *impossible to hear*.
c My great grandmother was completely *unable to read or write*.
d The minister's explanation was completely *unconnected with the question*.
e I don't know what the message says. The writing is *impossible to read*.
f They were very *unlucky* not to win.

Section A: Predicting what you will read

It makes it easier to read a text if you have some idea beforehand what you can expect it to be about.

Before you read the newspaper article on the opposite page, look at this reduced version. Read just the parts in large print, and try to guess the answers to these questions.

1 Will the article be mainly about the tree or mainly about the drug?

2 Why is the drug dangerous?

3 What do you think criminals do with it?

The tree that drives Colombians mad

A particularly insidious drug extracted from the tree *Datura arborea* is being exploited by criminals in Colombia. **Anne Proenza** reports from Bogotá.

When the Spanish discovered and invaded the savannah around Bogotá in the 17th century, they found the area covered with *Datura arborea*, a small tree with spectacular bell-shaped flowers. Legend has it that when they discovered the effects it had on anyone or any animal that rested for a moment beneath its branches they nicknamed it 'the tree that drives people mad'.

Today the *borrachero* (the common name for the tree) is still sending people out of their minds. In the seventies Colombian criminals discovered a way of extracting an alkaloid called scopolamine (or hyoscine) from part of its fruit. They used the alkaloid to make a devastating drug which has a 'hypnotic' effect on people and causes them to lose their memory.

Since then, the use of *burundanga* (the popular Colombian name for the drug and all its variants) has been on the increase. Two months ago, under its influence, a senator and his wife spent a whole night withdrawing large amounts of money from their various banks' cash dispensers and gave it to thieves. They then opened up their flat and handed over their most precious possessions to the gang.

But that was a relatively banal case of how the drug can be used for criminal purposes. Every weekend, 15–20 victims are admitted to the emergency ward of Bogotá's Kennedy Hospital with absolutely no recollection of what has happened to them. It usually turns out they have been robbed of their money and jewellery, and sometimes raped.

The drug responsible, made from scopolamine and/or benzodiazepine (a synthetic substance which goes into many tranquillisers, and which has similar effects to scopolamine when administered in high doses), seems to be a Colombian speciality that is only rarely used outside the country's borders.

Dr Camilo Uribe of the Bogotá Toxicology Clinic thinks that *burundanga* is responsible for over 80% of the poisoning cases that the casualty departments of Colombian hospitals have to deal with.

He says it is an ideal drug for criminals: 'The victim does what he or she is told, then forgets both what happened and who the attackers were. It's a perfect form of chemical "hypnosis" which allows all sorts of crimes.'

He recalls the case of a well-known diplomat who vanished on a Friday evening after having a drink at a swish Bogotá bar. He reappeared the following Tuesday, when he was arrested by customs

> **People mistrust any stranger who offers them something to eat or drink.**

officers at Santiago airport in Chile in the company of a woman he did not know – and in possession of two kilos of cocaine.

Scopolamine acts directly on the central nervous system. The effect of the drug on the brain is comparable to that of a power cut on a computer: all the data so far memorised is lost for ever.

Whether made of scopolamine (a natural substance) or benzodiazepine (an artificial substance), *burundanga* has to be administered orally to have an effect. It takes the form of a white or yellow powder which has the advantage, for the criminal, of being perfectly soluble and remaining odourless and tasteless.

There is only one way for people to avoid the dreaded effects of *burundanga*, and that is to mistrust any stranger who offers them something to drink or eat. Most cases of poisoning occur in nightspots or during public events.

The toxicology department of the Institute of Forensic Science has a display case filled with all the potential traps – sweets, chewing gum and pieces of chocolate containing the poison, some slightly cloudy *aguardiente* (the local spirit), and an unopened can of Coca-Cola into which the poison had been injected through a tiny hole.

Datura arborea still grows wild in Colombia and elsewhere in South America. For the past few years, there has been intensive farming of the tree in Ecuador to meet the needs of the pharmaceutical industry. It would seem that some of the substances produced find their way illegally into Colombia. Paradoxically, a superb specimen of the 'tree that drives people mad' is to be found in the courtyard of the Institute of Forensic Science in Bogotá.

Section B: Reading for the main idea

The first time you read a text, it is often useful to read it through quickly to get the main idea.

1 Read through the first four paragraphs of the article on the opposite page. Try to read fairly quickly, without using a dictionary, and find answers to the three questions in Section A.

2 Now read the rest of the text, again fairly quickly, and without using a dictionary. Which of these do you think are *main points*, and which are minor details?

 a Benzodiazepine is used in tranquillisers.

 b Burundanga is a perfect drug for criminals because the victim doesn't remember what happened afterwards.

 c Under the influence of the drug, the victim does whatever the criminal suggests.

 d Burundanga is sometimes injected into cans of Coca-Cola.

 e In Colombia, you should be very careful not to accept food or drink from strangers.

 f 80% of all poisoning cases in Colombia are caused by burundanga.

 g *Datura arborea* is farmed in Ecuador.

Section C: Finding specific information

Often we read a text in order to find out particular things we are interested in. For example, here are some notes that might be made by a pharmacologist, who is interested in the drug itself and what it consists of.

Make two sets of similar notes:

1 just about the tree, as if made by a botanist (where it grows, what it looks like, etc.)
2 just about the drug, as if made by a criminologist (what it looks like, how it is taken, what effect it has on the victim).

'Burundanga' (Colombian name)
– alkaloid, attacks central nervous system
– causes hypnosis and loss of memory

Two forms:
1. scopolamine – natural substance from fruit of Datura arborea
2. benzodiazepine – synthetic, used in tranquillisers

The tree that drives Colombians mad

A particularly insidious drug extracted from the tree *Datura arborea* is being exploited by criminals in Colombia. **Anne Proenza** reports from Bogotá.

When the Spanish discovered and invaded the savannah around Bogotá in the 17th century, they found the area covered with *Datura arborea*, a small tree with spectacular bell-shaped flowers. Legend has it that when they discovered the effects it had on anyone or any animal that rested for a moment beneath its branches they nicknamed it 'the tree that drives people mad'.

Today the *borrachero* (the common name for the tree) is still sending people out of their minds. In the seventies Colombian criminals discovered a way of extracting an alkaloid called scopolamine (or hyoscine) from part of its fruit. They used the alkaloid to make a devastating drug which has a 'hypnotic' effect on people and causes them to lose their memory.

Since then, the use of *burundanga* (the popular Colombian name for the drug and all its variants) has been on the increase. Two months ago, under its influence, a senator and his wife spent a whole night withdrawing large amounts of money from their various banks' cash dispensers and gave it to thieves. They then opened up their flat and handed over their most precious possessions to the gang.

But that was a relatively banal case of how the drug can be used for criminal purposes. Every weekend, 15–20 victims are admitted to the emergency ward of Bogotá's Kennedy Hospital with absolutely no recollection of what has happened to them. It usually turns out they have been robbed of their money and jewellery, and sometimes raped.

The drug responsible, made from scopolamine and/or benzodiazepine (a synthetic substance which goes into many tranquillisers, and which has similar effects to scopolamine when administered in high doses), seems to be a Colombian speciality that is only rarely used outside the country's borders.

Dr Camilo Uribe of the Bogotá Toxicology Clinic thinks that *burundanga* is responsible for over 80% of the poisoning cases that the casualty departments of Colombian hospitals have to deal with.

He says it is an ideal drug for criminals: 'The victim does what he or she is told, then forgets both what happened and who the attackers were. It's a perfect form of chemical "hypnosis" which allows all sorts of crimes.'

He recalls the case of a well-known diplomat who vanished on a Friday evening after having a drink at a swish Bogotá bar. He reappeared the following Tuesday, when he was arrested by customs

People mistrust any stranger who offers them something to eat or drink.

officers at Santiago airport in Chile in the company of a woman he did not know – and in possession of two kilos of cocaine.

Scopolamine acts directly on the central nervous system. The effect of the drug on the brain is comparable to that of a power cut on a computer: all the data so far memorised is lost for ever.

Whether made of scopolamine (a natural substance) or benzodiazepine (an artificial substance), *burundanga* has to be administered orally to have an effect. It takes the form of a white or yellow powder which has the advantage, for the criminal, of being perfectly soluble and remaining odourless and tasteless.

There is only one way for people to avoid the dreaded effects of *burundanga*, and that is to mistrust any stranger who offers them something to drink or eat. Most cases of poisoning occur in nightspots or during public events.

The toxicology department of the Institute of Forensic Science has a display case filled with all the potential traps – sweets, chewing gum and pieces of chocolate containing the poison, some slightly cloudy *aguardente* (the local spirit), and an unopened can of Coca-Cola into which the poison had been injected through a tiny hole.

Datura arborea still grows wild in Colombia and elsewhere in South America. For the past few years, there has been intensive farming of the tree in Ecuador to meet the needs of the pharmaceutical industry. It would seem that some of the substances produced find their way illegally into Colombia. Paradoxically, a superb specimen of the 'tree that drives people mad' is to be found in the courtyard of the Institute of Forensic Science in Bogotá.

7 Working it out

A Taking sides

Rewrite these opinions using *must* or *can't*, and add a reason using *If …* or *Otherwise …*
Examples:

> Of course aliens haven't visited the Earth. They haven't taken us over, have they?

Aliens can't have visited the Earth. If they had, they would have taken us over.

> We've been visited by aliens, I'm sure of that. There are so many UFO sightings.

We must have been visited by aliens. Otherwise, there wouldn't be so many UFO sightings.

> It's nonsense to say that the Earth's flat – no one's fallen off the edge, have they?

1 ....

> The Vikings didn't discover America. They don't speak Norwegian there, do they?

2 ....

> Of course the sun isn't cooling down. The Earth isn't getting cooler, is it?

3 ....

> Father Christmas exists, that's certain. The children get their presents, don't they?

4 ....

> A monster in Loch Ness? There isn't one! Where's the scientific evidence?

5 ....

> It's quite clear that Lord Lucan committed suicide. He's never been found, has he?

6 ....

Now choose one of the topics, and take the opposite point of view. Give at least one reason for your opinion.

....

....

....

....

B Appearance and the senses

Rewrite these sentences so that they mean the same. Use the words given.

Example:

This soup has a disgusting taste.

This soup tastes ....*disgusting.*..............

seem and appear		
He	seems appears	to like you. to be working late. to have left early.
'Sense' verbs		
She	looks sounds	tired. like a politician. as if she needs help.

1 It seems that they're enjoying themselves.

   They seem ....

2 From your voice, I'd say you have a cold.

   You sound ....

3 They've left the country, it appears.

   They appear ....

4 Those roses have got a beautiful smell.

   Those roses smell ....

5 She resembles her mother.

   She looks ....

6 As far as anyone can tell, they're very pleasant.

   They seem ....

C Reason and purpose

Here are some answers to the question *What made you decide to learn a foreign language?* **Choose those you think are the most important reasons, and write a paragraph about them. Add your own reasons if you like. Use expressions from the box where appropriate.**

One reason (why) …	… in order to …
The main reason …	… so as to …
Another reason …	… as a way of -ing …

It's a great way of meeting people.

I have to use Russian in my work.

We had to do two foreign languages at school.

It's a hobby with me – I just enjoy learning languages.

There are various reasons why people learn foreign languages.

....

....

....

....

....

....

....

....

I live in France now, so learning French was the obvious thing to do.

You can't really appreciate literature and poetry except in the original.

When I'm abroad, I want to be able to talk to people in their own language.

IDIOMS: Parts of the body (2)

Look at these sentences, and replace the underlined words using an idiom from the box.

1 I took a big risk leaving everything and going off to Brazil, but I <u>was very lucky</u> – I found a job, got married, and here I am.
2 She lost the match 5:0, but she <u>tried not to show her disappointment</u>.
3 He really <u>wants very much</u> to become an airline pilot, so I hope he passes the medical exam.
4 Could you <u>help me</u>? I can't get the video to work.
5 We sometimes disagree, but we <u>share the same point of view</u> about most things.
6 I was <u>thinking as hard as I could</u>, trying to remember where they lived.

lend someone a hand
set your heart on something
put a brave face on it
land on your feet
rack your brains
see eye to eye

LISTENING: Life elsewhere?

1 You will hear four people saying whether they believe there is life elsewhere in the universe.

Before you listen, check that you know what these words mean:

grain of sand	arrogant
statistically	evolve
inhabited	unidentified flying object

2 🔲 Listen to the recording. How many of the speakers believe that:
   a there is life elsewhere in the universe?
   b aliens have landed on the earth?

3 🔲 Which of the speakers makes these points? Listen again and write 1, 2, 3, 4 or – in Column A. In Column B, write ✓ or ✗ to show whether you agree or not.

	A	B
a The climate on other planets wouldn't allow life to evolve.		
b Aliens are making contact with us through stories we make up about them.		
c Beings on other planets live too far away to travel to Earth.		
d UFOs must come from somewhere in our own solar system.		
e It isn't likely that ours is the only planet that can support life.		
f There are probably other life forms that are more advanced than we are.		
g What we think are aliens are in fact beings visiting us from the future.		

COMMON VERBS: come

1 Apart from its basic meaning (= *arrive*), *come* is also used as part of other expressions.

Look at these sentences. Match the use of *come* with the paraphrases in the box.
   a The water nearly *came up to* my neck.
   b I *came to the conclusion* that she was lying.
   c Her job seems to *come before* her family.
   d In questions, the verb *comes* before the noun.
   e After many years, I *came to* understand her better.
   f 'Algebra' *comes from* an Arabic word meaning 'putting together'.
   g She's finding it hard to *come to terms with* the fact that she's lost her job.
   h At last the harbour *came into view*.
   i These bits of wood might *come in handy*.
   j Lipstick has *come* back *into fashion* this year.
   k Roberta *came* first in the 100 metres.
   l The bill *comes to* $45.20

She can't accept it.	We could see it.
That's how deep it was.	She was the winner.
It's more important.	That's its origin.
I could use them.	That's its position.
People are wearing it.	It happened slowly.
That's what I decided.	That's the total.

2 Here are some phrasal verbs with *come*. Do you know what they mean? If not, use a dictionary to find out.
   a I *came across* an interesting picture in that magazine.
   b Good jobs aren't easy to *come by* these days.
   c Why don't you *come round* and have a chat?
   d We argued for a long time, but eventually they *came round to* my point of view.
   e In the end, it *comes down to* money.

A The job for you?

Choose two of these jobs – one you think would be suitable for you, and one you think wouldn't be suitable for you. (If you like, you can choose jobs that are not in the list.)

Say what you would like and dislike about each job. Use the ideas in the box to help you.

shop assistant	office manager	writer	actor	salesperson
bus driver	electrician	journalist	teacher	disc jockey
architect	police officer	secretary	accountant	factory worker

pay
necessary skills
holidays
promotion
contact with people
variety
travel
taking orders
independence
responsibility
hours
smartness
personality

Example: shop assistant

I wouldn't want to be a shop assistant. You have to work long hours and the pay isn't very good. I'd certainly meet a lot of people, but I wouldn't be very good with the difficult customers: I'd probably lose my temper with them and get the sack. The other thing is that I don't dress particularly smartly, and I'm not very punctual, either.

1 *Job:* ....
....
....
....
....
....
....

2 *Job:* ....
....
....
....
....
....
....

B Business verbs

Here are some people talking about their businesses. Fill the gaps with appropriate forms of expressions in the box.

1 We did rather well last year. Our turnover .... by 25%, and we .... of around £25,000, so we were able to .... an extra member of staff.

2 Things are hard in the building trade at the moment. This year, unfortunately, we expect to .... , and if that happens we'll have to .... a number of employees.

3 Six months ago, we .... a bank loan of £30,000. If things go well, we should be able to .... the loan within a year.

4 I worked for an engineering company for 10 years, and when I .... three years ago I decided to .... my own business.

5 We don't expect to make any money from this deal, but with any luck, we'll manage to ....

| break even |
| lay off |
| make a loss |
| make a profit |
| make redundant |
| pay off |
| rise |
| set up |
| take on |
| take out |

C Selling the product

Imagine you've applied for a job with an advertising agency. As part of an aptitude test, you have to design an advertisement. Choose one of the products on pages 96–97 in the Classroom Book, and design an advertisement that does not break any of the Advertising Standards Authority's rules.

IDIOMS: Describing feelings

1 What feelings do these idioms describe? Match them with the words in the box.

    a I was *scared stiff*.
    b I felt *on top of the world*.
    c I was *at my wits' end*.
    d I was completely *at a loss*.
    e I was *up in arms* about it.
    f I felt rather *on edge*.

desperate	very happy
angry	nervous
terrified	unable to decide

2 Choose idioms to fill the gaps in these sentences.

    a Suddenly, a huge wave crashed over the boat. Mary was ....

    b He already owes money to the bank, and now he's lost his job. He's ....

    c Apparently they're planning to close the railway, and the whole village is ....

    d I wish the exam results would come. She's been .... all week.

    e It was a wonderful spring morning, and I was feeling ....

    f What on earth shall I get him for his birthday? I'm ....

LISTENING: The new design manager

1 🔲 You will hear a business meeting at which four people are discussing who to choose as a new design manager for their company. The candidates they discuss are:
– Sandra Cunningham   – Nick   – Lisa

Listen to the recording once, without trying to understand every word, and find answers to these questions.

    a Which candidates are already working for the company?
    b What seem to be the main strengths of each candidate?

2 🔲 Listen to the recording again, and look at these notes about the candidates. Which candidate(s) does each apply to? Is it a plus or a minus point for them as a candidate? Mark each one *S*, *N* or *L*, and + or –.

S/N/L	+ or –	
		happiest as part of a team
		reliable and stable
		lots of creative flair
		no direct design experience
		has been with the company for for a year
		three years as a project manager
		combines stability and creativity

3 What seems to be the main reason not to appoint:
– either Nick or Lisa?
– Sandra?

4 Who do you think will be appointed?

WORD BUILDING: Nouns and verbs (2)

1 The verb *invent* has two nouns that go with it:
Alexander Bell *invented* the telephone.
Alexander Bell was a famous Scottish *inventor*.
The telephone was a 19th century *invention*.

Use a dictionary to help you complete this table:

Verb	Noun (person)	Noun (abstract)
invent	inventor	invention
compete	competitor	competition
....	investigator	....
....	....	operation
translate	....	....
....	....	investment
employ	....	....
....	....	survival
....	applicant	....
....	robber	....

2 Fill the gaps with suitable words from the table.

    a My son won first prize in a poetry ....

    b The police are conducting an .... into the fire.

    c She .... all her money in diamonds.

    d I was one of 20 .... for the job.

    e Unfortunately, there were no .... from the plane crash.

3 Write two other words you know that end in:
    a -tion   *b* -or   *c* -ment   *d* -er

A Read the text below, and decide which word, *a*, *b*, *c* or *d* best fits each space. There is an example at the beginning (0).

Meeting old school friends again can be a strange experience. Some have changed so much that you can (0) … recognise them: they speak with a different (1) … , are interested in different things, and all you can do is make (2) … talk and hope they'll go soon. Others, though you might have been out of (3) … with them for years, are just the same as they always were – it's (4) … if you last saw them yesterday. Before you know it, you're exchanging (5) … about your families and friends, and setting out the (6) … for another game of chess. A few change for the better. There's one person that I get (7) … with very well now, though we weren't on speaking (8) … for our last two years at school. One day, we met at a party and made it (9) … , and (10) … engaged the same evening.

	a	*b*	*c*	*d*
0	nearly	almost	(hardly)	easily
1	language	accent	way	tongue
2	small	little	silly	gossip
3	sight	touch	sound	feel
4	just	like	so	as
5	words	speech	talk	gossip
6	counters	draughts	squares	pieces
7	on	off	up	down
8	relations	terms	situation	condition
9	on	off	up	down
10	came	went	got	made

B Read the text below and and think of the word that best fills each space. Use only *one* word in each space. There is an example at the beginning (0).

Over the last few decades, people's working lives (0) ....*have*............ changed dramatically. In the past, unless you were sacked for some reason, you expected to stay in the same job (11) .... quite a few years. Nowadays jobs are much less secure. As companies try to save as much money as they can, employees are (12) .... redundant in their thousands. The workers who replace them are forced to (13) .... contracts that last only one or two years. They are usually younger, and so (14) .... paid less money. It is not surprising, then, that many older people decide to (15) .... up their own small businesses instead of trying to (16) .... another job in someone else's. Being self-employed certainly has its advantages: you don't have to (17) .... orders from anyone else, and if you make a (18) ...., you can keep it all for yourself. On the other hand, if you have had no previous (19) .... of running your own business, it's very easy to make mistakes. One common mistake is to offer a service for which there is little or no demand. A business that (20) .... faulty TV sets, for example, is unlikely to do well in an area where most people rent their TVs rather than buy them.

C Complete the second sentence so that it has a similar meaning to the first. Use the word given and other words to complete each sentence. Use between two and five words. Do not change the word given.

Example: From their voices, I'd say they're having a serious argument.   **SOUND**

They ....*sound as if*....................... they're having a serious argument.

(You could write *sound as if* or *sound as though* in the space. Both are correct.)

21 'I didn't steal the money,' said Leo.   **DENIED**

Leo .... the money.

22 If you've got nothing else to do, come round for dinner.   **LOOSE**

If you're ...., come round for dinner.

23 I last went there five years ago. **BEEN**

I .... five years.

24 He never washes up, and that annoys me. **THING**

.... is the fact that he never washes up.

25 I only realised I'd been drugged when I tried to stand up. **UNTIL**

It .... to stand up that I realised I'd been drugged.

26 I thought he was very unpleasant. **SEEMED**

He .... to me.

27 What's the name of that actress? Her husband drowned in the bath. **WHOSE**

What's the name of that actress .... in the bath?

28 By tomorrow evening, they'll be in Budapest. **ARRIVED**

By tomorrow evening, ... in Budapest.

29 <u>Tolstoy</u> didn't write *The Brothers Karamazov*, did he? **WHO**

It .... *The Brothers Karamazov*, was it?

30 They haven't won the competition, because they haven't rung us. **WOULD**

If they'd won the competition, ... us.

31 Don't tell them anything. It's none of their business. **NOTHING**

Don't tell them anything. It's .... them.

32 It's possible that they didn't receive your letter. **MIGHT**

They .... your letter.

D Read the text below and look carefully at each line. Some of the lines are correct and some have a word which should not be there. If a line is correct, put a tick (✓) in the box at the end of the line. If a line has a word which should not be there, write the word in the box. There are two examples (0 and 00).

Last summer, I went to Rio de Janeiro to visit my cousin Rita. While	0 ✓
I was being there, we spent a lot of afternoons on the sandy beaches	00 *being*
near her apartment, which they were absolutely wonderful. Rita was	33
very good at surfing, and she gave me some lessons. One day I had	34
a really great ride: I must to have surfed for at least 20 metres before	35
I fell off. On the last day of the holiday, Rita offered me to take me	36
up Sugar Loaf Mountain, which you can see it from the balcony of	37
her apartment. So we bought a ticket and went up on the cable car.	38
Unfortunately, I'm afraid of the heights, and when I looked down	39
at the land and sea far below us, I was absolutely terrified: I had shut	40
my eyes for the rest of the trip, and didn't even take a photo. If I'd	41
have known what it would be like, I never would have gone.	42

E Use the word given in capitals at the end of each line to form a word that fits in the space in the same line. There is an example at the beginning (0).

Last month I entered a (0) ....*competition*........ to find the young **COMPETE**

(43) .... of the year. You had to send in a completed **INVENT**

(44) .... form, together with a diagram showing **APPLY**

details of your (45) .... and a handwritten **INVENT**

(46) .... of how it works. The judges complained that **EXPLAIN**

some of my handwriting was (47) .... They thought my **LEGIBLE**

idea for self-cleaning windows was very (48) .... , but **ORIGIN**

that it would be (49) .... for most people to replace all **PRACTICAL**

their windows. I think their comments were (50) .... **RIDICULE**

9 Possibilities

A Would it work?

Ten days a week?

It's time for a change, says Chris Huntley of the Decimal Time Society

BECAUSE HUMAN BEINGS have ten fingers, it is natural for us to think in tens. Our numbering system is based on ten, and we use decimals in all our calculations, whether we're studying mathematics or simply doing our shopping – using money which is based on ten and weights and measures which are also based on ten. This is an admirably simple system which we use for almost every aspect of our daily lives – except for time.

A crazy time system

Our time system is decidedly *not* simple. We can't help having 365 days in a year – that's a fact of life – but why do we have to group them into *twelve* months of different lengths, or into (just over) *fifty-two* weeks of *seven* days each? And during one of these days, how do we tell the time? By dividing the day into *twenty-four* hours, each of which contains *sixty* minutes, each of which contains *sixty* seconds. Not only that, instead of numbering the hours from one to twenty-four, we only use the numbers one to twelve, and then repeat them all over again. So it isn't enough just to say you're doing something at nine o'clock, because it isn't clear which nine o'clock you're talking about – the one in the morning or the one in the evening. The whole thing's crazy. How much simpler it would be if we adopted a time system based on ten.

A ten-hour day

Let's take the days first. Each day would be divided into just ten hours; each hour would contain 100 minutes, and each minute would contain 100 seconds. (This would, interestingly, give us decimal seconds that are only slightly shorter than the ones we have at the moment.)

You could then agree to meet a friend at, say, 7.75 (that is, 75 minutes past seven, or quarter to eight) and there would be no possible confusion about whether you meant morning or evening. And an hour and a half would not be 90 minutes, but a much more sensible 150 minutes – or 1.5 hours.

A ten-day week

Imagine beginning your year with a five-day New Year holiday. You'd then be quite ready for the first working day of the year – Day One of Week One.

Unlike the weeks we have now, it would last for ten days, and there would be exactly 36 weeks in the year. And in leap years, you'd simply get an extra day's holiday at New Year, instead of an extra day in February.

In fact, there would be no need for months at all. Dates would simply be numbers. Day 93, for example, would be three days into the tenth week – it could also be written 9.3: nine weeks plus three days. And the days of the week would need new names – 'See you on Fourday'.

Would it work?

Of course it would. There would be some difficulties to start with, of course, but as soon as people got used to the new system, its advantages would become obvious.

In 1971, Britain changed from a crazy currency (12 pence to a shilling, 20 shillings to a pound) to a sensible decimal system. Many predicted that it would cause chaos, yet a few months later, the old currency was forgotten. Changing to a sensible time system would be a very similar – and entirely beneficial – experience. ■

---

1 **Read the article and find answers to these questions.**

a In a decimal time system, there would be .... seconds in a minute, ... minutes in an hour, ... hours in a day, ... days in a week and .... weeks in a year.

b How would the year start? ....

c Write down two advantages of a decimal time system that the writer mentions.

....

2 **Think of two reasons why it might be difficult to change to a decimal time system. Use the ideas in the box to help you.**

....

....

....

tradition
religion
cost
education
work

B I'm not sure …

The speakers below are not sure what they are going to do.
Add a sentence beginning *It depends* … to explain why.

Example:
I might call in and see you on the way home.
(time?)

It depends on   whether I've got time.
                     how much time I've got.

Dependency
How many people visit the zoo at weekends?
It depends | on the weather. (on) what the weather's like. (on) whether it's a nice day or not.

1 I'm not sure whether I'm going on holiday this year or not. *(money?)*

....

2 I might not bother to have a cooked lunch today. *(hungry?)*

....

3 We might not be able to come tonight. *(babysitter?)*

....

4 I'm not sure what time we'll get there. *(traffic?)*

....

5 I might give you a call next week some time. *(busy?)*

....

C Probability

Rewrite these sentences using:

certain to   likely to   unlikely to
sure to
bound to

Probability expressions
bound They'll certainly win. → They're **certain to** win. **sure**
He'll probably arrive soon. → He's **likely to** arrive soon.
There probably won't be many people there. → **There are unlikely to be** many people there.

1 If you take care, you probably won't have any trouble.

....

2 I'm sure your friends will be hungry when they arrive.

....

3 The thief is probably someone employed by the company.

....

4 There's a supermarket somewhere near here, surely.

....

5 Rich people have a longer life expectancy than poor people.

....

6 I don't expect there will be too many insects at this time of year.

....

7 The Canadians will certainly do well in this year's championship.

....

IDIOMS: Streets and roads

Look at these sentences. See if you can guess from the context what the idioms in italics mean.

1 I know she likes inventing things, so I've bought her a book which should be *right up her street*. It's called '101 (Un)useless Japanese Inventions'.

2 They all speak good English, but Axel is *streets ahead* of the others. I think we should move him up into a higher class.

3 I soon realised that working in a supermarket was *a dead end*, so I went to evening classes and learned about computers.

4 Could you stop humming that awful tune? You're *driving me round the bend*!

5 It's a small restaurant right *off the beaten track* in a little village called Lacock, but they serve excellent food.

6 The best thing about living in Geneva is that you've got the Alps right *on your doorstep*, so in the winter you can go skiing every weekend.

Use a dictionary to check your answers.

LISTENING: Return from Berlin

You will hear a woman describing an incident at a railway station in Berlin. The recording is in three parts.

Part 1

🔲 Look at these key words and listen to the recording.

taxi driver – luggage – platform – train –

a nice little lad – suitcase – strange men

Using the words, write two or three sentences, summarising what the woman says.

Part 2

Here are some questions. Before you listen, try to guess what the answers might be.

a What did they take from her shoulder bag?
b What two choices did the woman have?
c What did she decide to do?
d What things had been stolen?
e What things hadn't been stolen?

🔲 Now listen and answer the questions.

Part 3

🔲 Listen and complete these sentences.

a Three hours later, she was waiting on the platform when she noticed ...
b As she got on the train, she saw ...
c So she ..., and said ...
d They ...
e This made her feel ...

COMMON VERBS: see

1 Apart from its basic meaning (e.g. *I saw them yesterday*), *see* is also used in other ways. Look at these examples. Match the use of *see* with the verbs in the box.

a Let's wait and *see* what she says.
b Do you *see* what the problem is?
c I'm not sure if I can help. I'll have to *see*.
d Somehow I can't *see* him settling down in a small village.
e *See* that you're there by 11 – I'll be waiting.
f I don't understand what she *sees* in him.
g Could I *see* you for a moment, please?
h I'll *see* you home, as it's so late.

find out	accompany
imagine	consider (it)
speak to	find attractive
be sure	understand

2 Here are some idiomatic expressions with the verb *see*. Do you know what they mean? If not, use a dictionary to find out.

a This coat has *seen better days*, but I still like it.
b I've been *seeing* quite *a lot of* Michael recently.
c At first I thought I was *seeing things*, but he really was wearing lipstick.
d We really ought to *see about* hiring a car.
e I'll be glad to *see the back of* him – I never liked him at all.
f She offered to *see* me *off* at the station.
g He pretended not to care, but everyone could *see through* that very easily.

10 Life, the universe and everything

A Five scientists

1 The text has five paragraphs, which talk about:

Galileo and astronomy	(G)
Charles Darwin and natural selection	(D)
Marie Curie and the discovery of radium	(C)
Albert Einstein and relativity	(E)
Alfred Wegener and continental drift	(W)

Before you read, look at these expressions. Which would you expect to find in which paragraph?

astronomer	evolved	radiation
atomic bombs	fault lines	revolves
earthquakes	mountains	species
element	mutations	time
energy	planets	uranium ore

Now read the text and check your answers.

2 **According to the text, which of these statements are true and which are false?**

a Galileo invented the telescope.

b Copernicus believed that the Earth moves round the Sun.

c After his arrest, Galileo realised that his theory was wrong.

d All mutations are harmful.

e Marie Curie discovered uranium.

f Marie Curie's work killed her.

g If you go for a trip in space, your watch will be slow when you get back.

h Einstein invented the atomic bomb.

i Africa was once part of Pangaea.

j The continents have stopped moving now.

In Galileo's time, the Church taught that the Earth was at the centre of the universe, and that all the other planets and stars, including the Sun, revolved around it. In 1609, hearing about the invention of a simple telescope, Galileo designed one himself, and used it to study the night sky. He realised that in fact the Earth revolves around the Sun (which had first been proposed by the Polish astronomer Nicolaus Copernicus in 1543), and published a book which proved it. He was arrested and tortured, and was forced to withdraw his theory. Afterwards, he was heard to say quietly to himself 'Yet it moves'.

After going on a scientific expedition to the Pacific, Charles Darwin formed his theory of natural selection, or 'the survival of the fittest'. According to the theory, random mutations take place within individuals in a species. Some mutations are harmful, and these individuals die. Others are beneficial – these individuals survive and pass on their new characteristics to their children. In this way, species are continually adapting to their environment. The theory claims that all species – including humans – evolved in this way from simple organisms, over a period of billions of years.

Interested in the recent discovery of radioactivity, Marie Curie noticed that that one particular kind of uranium ore produced an unusually large amount of radiation, and realised that it must contain a new element. She and her husband spent four years extracting one gram of radium from eight tons of uranium ore. For their discovery of radium, they were awarded the 1903 Nobel Prize for Physics. She died at the age of 67, as a result of the radiation to which she had been exposed.

Einstein's theory of relativity, which was first published in 1905 when he was 26, gave scientists a completely new way of looking at the universe. Dealing with light, motion, energy, gravity and time, it is not easy to understand, though some of its effects are. For example, the theory predicts that time will pass more slowly for someone travelling in space. The theory of relativity also made it possible to construct atomic bombs, and after the Second World War, Einstein actively campaigned against the use of nuclear weapons.

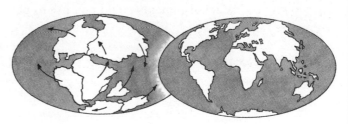

No-one believed Alfred Wegener in 1912 when he suggested that all the continents were once joined in one huge land mass called 'Pangaea', and have somehow moved apart over the last 200 million years. Now we know he was right: the continents are not fixed, but 'drift' slowly over the Earth's surface on huge 'plates'. The theory explains how mountains were formed: when two plates collided, one of them would rise up over the other – this is the reason that mountains tend to occur in 'chains' or long lines. Places where two plates come together are called 'fault lines', and these are where earthquakes occur. San Francisco lies on a major fault line. So does Japan.

B Environmental issues

Each box contains key words relating to an environmental issue. Choose two of the issues and write a short paragraph about each, using words from the box to help you, and adding any information you like.

Example:

spraying crops pesticides chemicals ban	*Nowadays most farmers spray their crops with pesticides and other chemicals. These kill insects and prevent plant diseases, but some are also harmful to the people who eat the crops. They also destroy wildlife. Some of the most dangerous chemicals have been banned, but not all of them, and not everywhere.*

1 ....
....
....
....

2 ....
....
....
....
....

greenhouse effect
fossil fuels
greenhouse gases
heat
trap
atmosphere
global warming

ozone layer
hole
CFCs (fridges)
protect
ultra-violet light
sun
skin cancer

nuclear power
radioactive waste
dangerous
store
thousands of
    years

destruction
habitat
species
extinct

C Believe it or not?

Look at the answers you gave in the *Beyond Science?* exercise (Classroom Book, p. 53), and choose one issue that interests you. What arguments could you use to persuade someone that you're right?

Magic powers   Fortune telling   Ghosts   Astrology   Psychokinesis

Reincarnation

Superstition

Telepathy

....
....
....
....
....
....
....
....

IDIOMS: Things people say

What do you think the idioms in italics mean? Choose *a* or *b*.

1 I'd just like to *put you in the picture* about my relationship with Peter.
   a I'd like to explain how things are.
   b I'd like to show you some photos.

2 They spent most of the evening *talking shop*.
   a They talked about money.
   b They talked about their work.

3 When I was talking to Pam last night, I'm afraid I rather *put my foot in it*.
   a I lost my temper with her.
   b I said something I shouldn't have.

4 I *couldn't get a word in edgeways* during the meeting.
   a Everyone was talking so much that I didn't have a chance to speak.
   b I couldn't think of anything to say.

5 Her name's *on the tip of my tongue*.
   a I can't quite remember her name.
   b I can't stop talking about her.

6 I'd like to *pick your brains* about video recorders.
   a I want to tell you about them.
   b I want to get information from you about them.

If you're not sure of the meaning, look up the idioms in a dictionary.

LISTENING: Reading the tarot

A   B   THE EMPRESS.

1 **You will hear someone telling a person's fortune from tarot cards. Before you listen, look at the two tarot cards. Which of them do you think might represent these things?**

balance between opposites	new knowledge
the feminine principle	a new beginning
creativity and rebirth	peace and harmony

2 Listen to what the woman says about card A. **Which of the things in the list does it represent?**

Complete these sentences:

Up to now, there have been … in the person's life.
Now she is starting to … , and to find … .

3 Listen to what the woman says about card B. **Which of the things in the list does it represent?**

Complete these sentences:

There's going to be a … in the person's life.
She's going to break free from … , and go through a period of … .

4 **Here are some things that happened to the woman soon afterwards. Do they fit what the tarot said?**

   a She left home and went to live with friends.
   b She had a serious argument with her parents.
   c She got a new job as a furniture designer.

WORD BUILDING: Adjectives and nouns (2)

1 **Nouns that come from adjectives often have one of these endings:**

| -(i)ty | -ence/ance | -th |
| -ness | -ency/ancy | |

Look at these examples. What adjective does each noun come from?

-(i)ty	-ence/ance	-th
possibility	patience	length
safety	importance	depth

-ness	-ency/ancy
darkness	urgency
laziness	pregnancy

2 **In these sentences, all the nouns in italics end in -ness, but only some are correct. Change the others into the correct form, using a dictionary to help you.**

   a I admire so many things about her: her *generousness*, her *intelligentness*, and above all her *self-confidentness*.
   b Weightlifting not only increases your *strongness* but also improves your general physical *fitness*.
   c I don't think you realise the *complexness* of this problem.
   d How well plants grow depends on the *humidness* of the air and on the *fertileness* of the soil.
   e Swiss train services are well known for their *efficientness* and *punctualness*.
   f The two things I hate most are *laziness* and *stupidness*.

D Study skills: Summarising information

Section A: Taking notes

1 You will hear someone talking about designing green roofs for buildings in cities.

Listen to the first part and look at these two sets of notes. Why is set B better than set A? Complete the notes in B for points 3 and 4.

A

Green roofs are becoming more popular.

Too many problems 10 years ago.

No technology to build them well.

No problems nowadays, many advantages.

Ecological advantages, keeps rainwater back.

Improves climate of cities.

Cooler than concrete.

Insulation against noise.

Thick layer of soil on roof.

B

Green roofs in cities

10 years ago : too many problems
 - no technology to build them well

Now : no problems
Advantages
1. ecological
    - keeps rainwater back
    - improves climate in cities
       (cooler than concrete in summer)
2. insulation against noise
    (thick layer of soil on roof)

3.

4.

48   *Study skills D*

2 📼 Listen to the second part of the recording, and take notes under these headings:

Looking after green roofs	Possible problems
Depends on type of green roof: 1. 2.	1. Technical 2. Cost

Section B: Writing a summary

1 Here is a 90-word summary of the information in the first part of the recording. Compare it with the notes opposite. Which of these has been added?
   – factual information
   – ways of joining sentences
   – ways of making the information clearer

> Green roofs in cities
>
> Ten years ago, many people were suspicious of green roofs, because there seemed to be too many problems connected with them. Now technology is more developed and these problems have been resolved.
>
> Green roofs have several advantages. The most important are ecological ones: green roofs hold back rainwater that would otherwise be wasted, and because they are cooler than concrete roofs they improve the climate of cities in the summer. As they have a thick layer of soil, green roofs also help to insulate buildings against noise.

Add one or two more sentences to the summary to cover your notes for points 3 and 4. Try not to write more than 20–25 words.

2 Write a summary of around 100 words based on your notes from the second part of the recording.

....

....

....

....

....

....

....

....

....

11 Evaluating

A Then and now

Look at these remarks, in which some elderly people are reminiscing about the way things were when they were children, and rewrite them using time comparison structures.

Time comparison structures

People used to go out more often than they do now.
People don't go out as often as they used to.

The streets are more dangerous than they used to be.
The streets aren't as safe as they used to be.
The streets used to be safer than they are now.

1 ....
....

2 ....
....

3 ....
....

4 ....
....

5 ....
....

In those days, you hardly saw a car in the street. Nowadays you're lucky to be able to find a parking place …

We used to go to the cinema twice a week. These days, of course, people have TV …

When I was a child, the trains used to leave every 20 minutes, not every hour …

There used to be 50 of us in a class. My grandson's class hasn't even got 30 in it …

We only used to have meat at weekends. Nowadays I eat meat twice a day …

B Giving advice

Imagine that some friends from abroad are about to visit your country for the first time. They want to know about:

– places to visit (and not to visit)
– what to bring with them (and not to bring with them)
– what to take home as souvenirs (and not to take home as souvenirs).

Give them some advice, using the structures in the box. If you like, add some reasons as well.

It's a good idea to …
It isn't a good idea to …
It's (well) worth …
It's not worth …
There's no point in …

....
....
....
....
....
....
....
....
....
....

C Good and bad effects

The diagram shows a proposed scheme for making changes to a town centre.

Below are the reactions of some local people to the scheme. Write about the effects the scheme will have, using the verbs given.

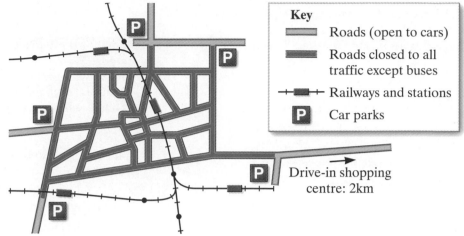

1 'I'll be able to do all my shopping at the same time.'
   ENABLE
   The scheme will enable people
   ....

2 'I won't be able to drive to work any more.'
   PREVENT
   It'll prevent
   ....

3 'People won't want to shop in the town centre if they can't bring their cars in.'
   DISCOURAGE
   ....

4 'I won't have to sit in rush-hour queues any more.'
   SAVE
   ....

5 'If the buses and trains are going to be cheaper and more frequent, I'm very happy to use them.'
   ENCOURAGE
   ....

6 'Now I'm going to have to drive for miles just to do a bit of shopping.'
   FORCE
   ....

7 'Getting around the centre will be much easier for pedestrians, without all those cars getting in the way.'
   MAKE IT EASIER
   ....

Now imagine you're a resident, a shopkeeper or an office worker. Write part of a letter to a local newspaper, either supporting or attacking the scheme.

....

....

....

....

....

....

....

....

....

IDIOMS: Other people

Use a dictionary to help you answer these questions.

1 Alex has got *a soft spot for* you. This means that:
   a he likes you
   b he's in love with you
   c you get on his nerves.

2 Marta *leaves you cold*. This means that:
   a you find her rather frightening
   b you're completely indifferent to her
   c she always ignores you.

3 Which of these three people would you want as friends? Why?
   – John, who *gets your back up*
   – Matilda, who *gives you the creeps*
   – Diana, who seems to be *on the same wavelength* as you

4 Someone said something to you which *made your blood boil*. This means that it made you:
   a wild with excitement
   b very frightened
   c very angry.

LISTENING: Panel discussion

You will hear a radio panel discussion about Third World charities, with a presenter and three speakers. Listen and answer the questions.

1 What does each speaker think about giving money to Third World charities? Write *A*, *B* or *C* in the table.

It's something everyone should do.	
In general, it's worthwhile.	
In general, it isn't worth it.	
There's absolutely no point in it.	

2 Which of these points do the speakers make? Write *A*, *B*, *C* or – beside each statement.

   a The West's efforts to help the Third World have often led to disaster.
   b Many people in the West give money to charities because they feel guilty.
   c The West has no right to tell the Third World what to do.
   d You shouldn't give money to charities unless you know how it's going to be used.
   e The West has so much money that they have a duty to give some to the Third World.
   f Money given to the Third World is often wasted.
   g It's worth spending money on educating people, so that they can help themselves.

3 Here are some expressions the speakers use. What do they mean? Use a dictionary if you need to.

   a how much of it goes in corruption
   b well-meaning people
   c with the best of intentions
   d tampering with water systems

COMMON VERBS: take

1 The verb *take* is used with several different meanings, and is often used in phrasal verbs. Look at these sentences, and match the uses of *take* with the paraphrases in the box.

   a The rebels *took* more than 100 prisoners.
   b I *took up* judo this year.
   c I didn't *take in* what she was saying.
   d I *take back* what I said to you just now.
   e It *took* us ten days to cross the Gobi Desert.
   f *Take* two tablets three times a day.
   g I didn't really *take to* his new girlfriend.
   h Who's *taken* my dictionary?
   i I *take after* my mother more than my father.
   j The phone *takes* either coins or cards.
   k I *took* her address and phone number.

It's missing.	They captured them.
I didn't mean it.	Swallow them.
I started doing it.	You can use either.
It was a long journey.	I wrote them down.
I didn't like her.	I wasn't concentrating.
I'm like her.	

2 Here are some idiomatic expressions with *take*. Do you know what they mean? If not, use a dictionary to find out.

   a There's no need to *take offence*, just because I asked you to be quiet.
   b I don't think he *takes* his job very *seriously*.
   c Her question *took me* completely *by surprise*.
   d I just *took it for granted* that he'd pay back the money.
   e Are you *taking part in* the race or just watching?
   f There's no hurry – just *take your time*.

12 Yourself and others

A Personality adjectives

This wordsearch puzzle contains 21 personality adjectives. Most of the answers appear in Exercise 12.1 in the Classroom Book, pages 62 and 100. The first letter of each answer is given.

Find words to describe people who:

1 look on the bright side of life (three answers)

P .... *positive* ....

O ....

C ....

2 are (too) interested in what other people are doing (two answers)

I ....

N ....

3 spend a lot of time thinking (two answers)

T ....

R ....

4 think about themselves too much (two answers)

S ....

V ....

5 enjoy talking to other people (two answers)

C ....

S ....

6 are afraid of other people (three answers)

I ....

S ....

T ....

7 are likely to attack other people

A ....

C	I	T	S	I	M	I	T	P	O	T	H	Y
A	O	I	Y	S	O	N	U	O	S	H	W	D
L	D	M	V	P	O	Q	F	S	O	O	E	S
M	A	I	M	X	I	U	Q	I	C	U	L	C
Z	G	D	S	U	S	I	P	T	I	G	B	H
E	G	Y	H	S	N	S	L	I	A	H	A	E
H	R	O	Y	A	N	I	A	V	B	T	N	E
S	E	U	E	V	I	T	C	E	L	F	E	R
I	S	I	C	U	Q	I	I	A	E	U	M	F
F	S	E	K	E	U	V	D	M	T	L	A	U
L	I	T	J	B	S	E	V	O	Y	I	X	L
E	V	I	T	I	S	N	E	S	R	E	V	O
S	E	A	S	Y	G	O	I	N	G	G	W	E

8 are easily upset

O ....

9 are not easily upset (four answers)

E ....

P ....

C ....

A ....

10 are unhappy unless everything is exactly right

F ....

Now write a brief description of your own personality, including at least two of the words from the puzzle.

....

....

....

....

....

....

....

....

....

B Laura's dream

1 Here is an account of a dream, taken from a book about interpreting dreams. Read the information about the person who had the dream, and then read about her dream.

In its interpretation, the book links parts of the dream to Laura's real life. Decide which parts of the dream you expect to be linked to the following:

a Laura was reluctant to take the job in the factory.
b She was feeling depressed.
c She was feeling ashamed.
d She was feeling angry.
e Her hopes had faded away …
f … but there was still hope for the future.
g The job would give her enough money to survive.
h She had lots of problems …
i … and she couldn't cope with them.
j Her financial situation was getting worse.
k She knew she'd find it difficult to keep up with the other workers in the factory.
l She wanted to paint again.

Now look at the interpretation from the book on page 74. How similar is it to yours?

2 What do you see as the main message of the dream? Summarise it in one or two sentences.

Now look at the interpretation from the book on page 74.

~ ABOUT LAURA ~

Laura had for a long time been working very happily as an artist, but had been able to sell only a few paintings. Money became scarce, and when her boyfriend lost his job they slipped deeper into debt. At the time of the dream she was being forced into taking a dull job in a factory. She knew that she would hate the job, but it was essential that she earned some money.

~ LAURA'S DREAM ~

❝I was about to get married, and was walking down the aisle. However, I was dressed entirely in black, with heavy black shoes and a black veil, and was carrying a bouquet of dead, black roses. I did not want to get married, and seemed neither to know nor care who the bridegroom was.

Suddenly, the aisle of the large and crowded church began to slope, so that I began to walk faster and faster towards the altar, despite my efforts to hang back. Reluctant and full of fear, I tried to keep away from the altar, which I now saw was piled high with dirty washing and a huge mound of earthy potatoes. I knew that I would have to do the washing and peel the potatoes.

The slope of the aisle now became even steeper, and all the people in the church began to chant 'Go, go, go!' As I approached the altar I dropped my bouquet, which then burst into hundreds of different things: saucepans, a shovel, socks, pieces of paper and all kinds of rubbish. The crowd shouted at me to clear up the mess so that they could all go home, and people started to poke me with long, skinny fingers. I tried to pick everything up, but it was difficult – the rubbish was suddenly blowing around and away from me. Then I caught a glimpse of a colourful butterfly; I reached out for it, but it flew up into the sky.❞

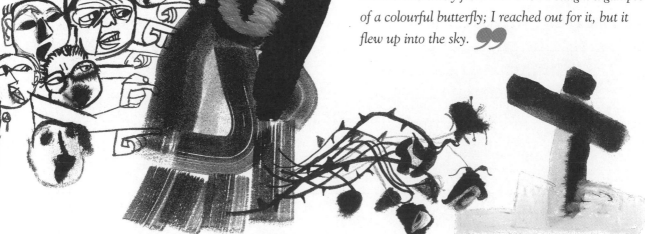

IDIOMS: Reactions

Look at these sentences, and replace the underlined words using an idiom from the box.

1 The caretaker knew that some students were staying out after midnight, but he decided to <u>pretend that he hadn't noticed</u>.

2 You shouldn't <u>take</u> what he said <u>so seriously</u> – he only meant it as a joke.

3 She decided that the time had come for her to <u>say exactly what she thought</u>, so she went to the manager's office and knocked on the door.

4 They were planning to sell their house and move to Canada, but at the last minute, they <u>lost courage</u> and decided to stay.

5 You can't let the children just do whatever they like. It's time you <u>took firm action</u> and told them to behave themselves.

6 It <u>feels unnatural</u> for me to complain about things, but the service is so bad that I've got to say something.

turn a blind eye to something
put your foot down
go against the grain
take something to heart
get cold feet
speak your mind

LISTENING: Two jokes

1 🔲 **You will hear two jokes about relationships. Listen to them in turn, and each time there is a pause in the recording, try to guess which of the two lines below will come next. Then try to guess the last line of the joke.**

Joke A

1 *a* to a young woman from a neighbouring farm.
　b to a woman he'd met through a dating agency.
2 *a* the woman suddenly burst into tears.
　b the horse stumbled.
3 *a* 'That's one!'
　b 'That's how I'll be in a few years' time!'
4 *a* He told the woman to get out and walk beside the wagon.
　b He got out his rifle and shot the horse dead.
5 The last line?

Joke B

1 *a* 'Excuse me, sir, I wonder if you would be so kind as to tell me what time it is?'
　b 'Excuse me, sir, could you give me £5?'
2 *a* 'You leave me alone!'
　b 'It's nearly two o'clock.'
3 *a* you'll probably ask me for money.
　b we'll get into a conversation.
4 *a* Then I'll probably invite you to stay the night.
　b At home I have a beautiful daughter.
5 The last line?

2 **What do you think the jokes are about? Choose two items from the list that best apply to each.**

envy	domination of women
jealousy	anxiety about money
cruelty	materialistic attitudes
loneliness	lack of communication
hospitality	control over other people
meanness	old-fashioned attitudes

WORD BUILDING: Prefixes (2)

1 **We saw in Prefixes (1) that *un-* and *in-* mean *not*, so *unlikely* means *not likely*. Which of the meanings in the box do these prefixes have?**

*mis*understand, *mis*take
*dis*agree, *dis*honest
*over*tired, *over*cook
*under*paid, *under*developed
*re*paint, *re*wind

too much
again, back
not enough
not, the opposite of
in the wrong way

2 **Find single words to replace the expressions in italics. Use a dictionary to help you.**

a I *slept too long* and missed the bus.
b Don't you dare *behave badly* in a restaurant again!
c She's *not at all satisfied* with her working conditions.
d He *doesn't approve* of people with tattoos.
e I've made so many corrections that I think I'll *write* the whole page *again*.
f You *interpreted* what I said *in the wrong way*.
g We're trying to help children *who are not as privileged as others*.

3 **The meaning of some words with these prefixes is not so obvious. Use a dictionary to find out what these phrases mean.**

a a misguided person　　*d* to overestimate
b to have a miscarriage　*e* an understatement
c to feel disillusioned

E Study skills: Developing a piece of writing

Section A: Jotting down ideas

1 If we have to write something, it is often useful to start by jotting down ideas. There is no 'right' way to do this: it depends on the way we think and on what we are writing about. The 'best' way is whatever way we find most helpful.

Here are three different kinds of notes for a short text about cross-country skiing.

A Brain-storming. The writer just jotted down all the ideas that came to mind.

> **C-C Skiing**
>
> Not as popular as downhill skiing.
> Not so exciting – like jogging.
> Good way to keep fit.
> Cheaper – no lifts, no equipment.
> You need a track (snow must be compressed like ice).
> Move by kicking back on skis.
> Skis long, thin, fastened at front only.
> Easiest to ski on flat ground.

B An outline. The writer tried to think of how to organise the text, and made brief notes.

> **C-C Skiing**
>
> Differences from downhill skiing:
> – not so exciting
> – not so popular
>
> Advantages:
> – healthy (uses all muscles)
> – cheaper
> – environment (narrow tracks)
>
> Skis:
> – long, thin
> – fixed at front only

C A diagram. The writer has thought of different areas, and made brief notes about each of them.

> **C-C Skiing**
>
> **cf. downhill skiing**
> – not so popular
> – cheaper
> – keeps you fitter
> – better for environment
>
> **Technique**
> Skis fixed at front
> – walking movements
> – kick backwards
> – about 10 kph
>
> **Tracks**
> Usually flat ground
> Made by other people or machines

2 Try this experiment. Choose a topic that you know something about (anything you like – it could be a hobby, your favourite writer or painter, an issue you feel strongly about, something you've studied at school or university). Jot down a few notes in the way you find most natural. Which of the three styles above was it most similar to?

Now make the same notes, but use one of the other styles. Did you notice any difference? Was it easier / more difficult? Did it help you more / less to organise your ideas?

Section B: Writing a draft and making improvements

1 Here is a rough draft made from the notes. Consider these points:

   a Could some of the ideas be made clearer or expanded?

   b Could some of the ideas be joined together better?

   c Could the overall shape of the writing be improved? (What's wrong with the ending?)

> Cross-country skiing is not as popular as downhill skiing. It isn't as exciting – it's more like going jogging on skis. It's a very good way to keep fit, because you use all the muscles in your body. It is much cheaper than downhill skiing because you don't have to pay for lifts. Also, you don't need so much special equipment. It's also better for the environment.
>
> Cross-country skis are longer and thinner than normal skis. They are fixed on at the toe, and you can walk on them. To move forward, you have to kick back on the ski. You can usually reach a speed of about 10 k.p.h. You have to ski along a track, which can either be made by other people or by a special machine. Usually the track goes over flat ground.

2 Here is an improved version of the same piece of writing. What has the writer done about the points you considered above?

> Cross-country skiing is not as popular as downhill skiing, probably because it isn't as exciting. It's more like going jogging on skis and, like jogging, it is a very good way to keep fit – in fact, it's one of the few sports in which you use nearly all the muscles in your body.
>
> Cross-country skis are longer and thinner than normal skis, and they are fixed only at the toe. To move forward, you have to kick back on the ski, and you can usually reach a speed of about 10 k.p.h. To move at a reasonable speed, you need a track, which can either be made by other people's skis or by a special machine.
>
> As well as keeping you fit, cross-country skiing has other advantages over downhill skiing. It's much cheaper (because you don't have to pay for lifts and you don't need so much special equipment), and it's also better for the environment – to go cross-country skiing you just need a narrow track which can go along existing footpaths.

3 Write a rough draft from your own notes.

   Look at it carefully, and ask yourself the same questions as those above.

   Then try to improve what you have written.

13 Right and wrong

A They were all to blame

Read these newspaper stories, and talk about the things that the different people involved did wrong or were doing wrong. Use an appropriate form of *should*.

Past forms of 'should'		
You	should have shouldn't have	taken the money. been listening. been punished.

1 The boy ....
....
....

2 The driver ....
....
....

3 The authorities ....
....
....

4 The boy's parents ....
....
....

Boy hit by car while playing in street

A NINE-YEAR-OLD BOY was taken to hospital with minor head injuries last night after being knocked down by a car while playing in the street outside his apartment block. The accident happened as the boy ran out into the road to fetch his ball.

Don Knight, the boy's father, said, 'It was the driver's fault – he was going too fast, and he wasn't looking where he was going. But I blame the authorities, too. We've asked them time and time again either to put up a sign saying SLOW – CHILDREN PLAYING, or else to provide a safe fenced-off play area. Perhaps now they'll take some action.'

MAN TAKES REVENGE ON NOISY NEIGHBOURS

When 38-year-old Thomas Kent's neighbours refused to turn their TV down at two o'clock in the morning, he phoned the police.

Half an hour later, the police had not arrived, so Mr Kent went to the apartment of pensioners George and May Tyler and asked them again to turn the sound down. When the couple (who are both hard of hearing) refused, he burst into the house and put his foot through their TV. By the time the police finally arrived, he had also smashed a CD player, three radios and a second TV.

Mr Kent's wife said later, 'This has been going on for months. We know they're slightly deaf, but they don't have to watch TV at that time of night. We've tried everything – we even bought them two sets of TV headphones, but they don't use them.'

Mr Kent spent yesterday being questioned by police.

5 The Tylers ....
....
....
....

6 Mr Kent ....
....
....
....

7 The police ....
....
....
....

B Could, should, needn't and might

Rewrite the sentences in italics using *could have*, *should have*, *needn't have* or *might have*.

1 They must have been crazy to swim out so far. *They ran the risk of drowning.*

     They could have drowned.

2 *It was a waste of my time making all those sandwiches.* They had plenty of food there already.

3 Why didn't you come by train? *It would have been easy for me to meet you at the station.*

4 *Why didn't you tell me you were eating out?* I've just cooked you a meal!

5 *It wasn't necessary for him to be so rude.* They were only trying to be helpful.

6 I'm surprised they only fined her. *She deserved to be sent to prison.*

7 You should have worn a stocking over your face. *You were in danger of being recognised.*

C Contrasting ideas

What is your view of the pairs of opinions below? Write the beginning of a paragraph.

Example:
Money spent on space travel could be better spent on other things. – Research into space travel has brought us many benefits.

Possible answers:
It may be true that there are more important things to spend money on than space research. On the other hand, most people would agree that it has brought us many benefits.

Many people think that research into space travel has brought us many benefits. In fact, however, the money would be far better spent on other things.

It simply isn't true that money spent on space travel would be better spent on other things. On the contrary, space research has brought us many benefits.

1 Vegetarians are healthier than meat-eaters. – Meat contains nutrients which are essential for good health.

2 Computers are an essential educational tool. – Some children waste all their time playing computer games.

If you like, develop one of the answers into a full paragraph, adding any arguments you think appropriate.

IDIOMS: All in the mind

What do you think the idioms in italics mean? Choose *a* or *b*.

1 I tried sailing, but I could never *get the hang of* it.
  a I couldn't see how to do it properly.
  b I couldn't see the point of it.

2 I asked him to get a fire going, but as usual he *got hold of the wrong end of the stick*.
  a He completely misunderstood what I told him.
  b He burned his fingers.

3 If you think I took your money, you're *barking up the wrong tree*.
  a You're crazy.
  b You're making a mistake.

4 Let's stop this conversation – we're *talking at cross purposes*.
  a We're making each other angry.
  b We're misunderstanding each other.

5 He's called Angelo – does that name *ring a bell*?
  a Does it sound nice?
  b Does it remind you of anything?

6 You don't have to *take* what she says *at face value*.
  a Don't believe what she says.
  b What she says isn't worth listening to.

If you're not sure of the meaning, look up the idioms in a dictionary.

LISTENING: Mistakes

1 **You will hear two stories about mistakes people made. Before you listen, use a dictionary to find out what these colloquial expressions mean.**

  – a gang of *rowdy* students
  – trying to *gate-crash* our party
  – I was absolutely *knackered*
  – someone *nicked* all my *stuff*

2   **Listen to the beginning of each story. Look at the questions below, and try to guess what the answers are.**

Story A

  a What did the gate-crasher try to do?
  b What did the speaker do?
  c What happened to the gate-crasher's thumb?
  d Why did the woman think he was lying?
  e Why was it 'embarrassing'?
  f How did she try to make up for it?
  g What did his thumb look like the next day?
  h Why did she feel guilty?

Story B

  a Why didn't the speaker want to get up?
  b Where did he decide to put the key so that the workman could get in?
  c Where was his flat?
  d What did his flat-mate tell him next morning?
  e How had the burglar got in?
  f What had the burglar stolen?

  Now listen to the two stories and answer the questions.

COMMON VERBS: put

1 *Put* **is used in English as a 'general purpose' verb, to talk about actions of various kinds. Look at these examples. What verb would be used in your own language to express the same meaning?**

  a *Put* some more wood on the fire – it's going out.
  b I haven't *put* any sugar in your coffee.
  c Where shall I *put* my coat?
  d I think I'll *put* a hat on – it's cold.
  e *Put* a full stop at the end of the sentence.
  f It's nearly time to *put* the children to bed.
  g The scandal *put* the Prime Minister in a very difficult position.
  h They're *putting* pressure on him to resign.

2 *Put* **is often used in phrasal verbs. Replace the words in italics with phrasal verbs from the box.**

put … off	put … down to
put … up	put up with
put … down	put across

  a I can't *tolerate* these living conditions any longer.
  b He always tries to *delay* things until the last minute.
  c Don't forget, if you're ever in London, I can *let you stay* in my flat.
  d She started behaving very strangely, but we all *believed it was caused by* stress at work.
  e Don't *humiliate* me in front of other people.
  f Have you seen this report about chickens? It really *discourages you from* eating eggs.
  g She manages to *communicate* complex ideas in a very simple way.
  h What a great book – I couldn't *stop reading* it.

14 Body and mind

A Talking about diseases

Look at the clues and write the missing words in the spaces on the right. If you're right, the circled letters in each answer should be the same.

All the answers are in the texts accompanying Exercise 14.1 in the back of the Classroom Book.

1 The main .... shown by sufferers of rabies is fear of water.

2 Aids is a relatively recent .... , but one which has spread rapidly around the world.

3 You can treat people who have just been bitten, but once rabies has .... , there is no cure.

4 The treatment for rabies involves a course of 17 ....s in the stomach wall.

5 People and their pets can be ....d against rabies.

6 The female anopheles mosquito passes the malarial .... from one human to another.

7 One way of protecting yourself from malaria is to wear insect ....

8 Because cholera is caused by a bacterium, it can be treated with ....

9 Scientists are conducting a huge amount of .... into finding out more about Aids.

10 A person can become .... with cholera by drinking contaminated water.

11 Cholera causes severe .... and vomiting.

12 Aids is passed on by sexual .... and the use of shared needles for injecting drugs.

13 The HIV virus attacks the body's .... system.

14 Malaria sufferers have a high temperature, or ....

15 The people most likely to die from malaria are children and .... women.

16 To avoid getting cholera, drink only water that has been boiled or .... with chlorine or iodine.

Now use the circled letters from answers 1–16 to complete this sentence.

People with any of these diseases need

B The man who was dead

Use the words in the box to fill the gaps in this joke. One of the words is used twice.

A man walked into a doctor's .... and announced that he was dead. The doctor did everything he could to persuade his .... that he was in fact alive: he took his .... (which was 36° – too warm for a dead man), he gave him a thorough medical .... (everything seemed to be working) and even gave him a chest .... (which showed nothing abnormal). But the man still insisted that he was dead. The doctor decided that the best thing to do was to give the man a .... for some tranquillisers and make an .... for him to see a .... But first, he thought he'd have one more try. 'Look,' he said, 'dead men don't .... , do they?' 'Of course not,' replied the man. 'Right,' said the doctor, and he took a surgical knife and stuck the point into the man's arm. .... flowed from the wound. 'Hmm,' said the man. 'I was wrong. Dead men *do* ....'

> appointment
> bleed
> blood
> examination
> patient
> prescription
> psychiatrist
> surgery
> temperature
> x-ray

C Homeopathy

1 Which of these questions does the text answer?

a Is homeopathy a recent development in medicine?

b If homeopathic medicines are made from poisons, aren't they dangerous?

c Could I give homeopathic medicines to my dog?

d Has anyone proved scientifically that homeopathic medicines work?

e Someone once told me that homeopathy aims to treat 'the whole person'. Is that true?

f Are there any diseases that homeopathic medicines can't be used for?

2 Look at these words in the text. What do you think they mean? Use a dictionary to check if you were right.

a *conventional* medicine

b *flushed* skin and *hallucinations*

c an *upset* stomach

d a single *remedy*

e the *dose* is extremely small

f *paradoxically*

Homeopathy is an alternative system of medicine that was developed in the early 19th century by Doctor Samuel Hahnemann. It is different from conventional medicine in several ways.

The law of similars

Everyone knows that cutting up an onion makes your eyes and nose run – in other words, it produces the symptoms of having a cold. Similarly, if you eat the poisonous plant *belladonna*, it gives you a hot, dry, flushed skin and hallucinations – both of which can occur in scarlet fever. It was observations like these that gave Dr Hahnemann the central idea of homeopathy: if onions gave a healthy person the symptoms of a cold, perhaps they could cure a person who was actually suffering from a cold. And perhaps substances like *belladonna*, which are normally poisonous, could be used to cure diseases with similar symptoms, like scarlet fever.

The single medicine

If you go to a conventional doctor with a headache, a sore throat and an upset stomach, you might come away with three different medicines. A homeopath, on the other hand, will conduct quite a long interview to find out all of your symptoms – mental and emotional as well as physical – and then prescribe a single remedy to deal with them all. The doctor might also recommend changes in diet and lifestyle as part of the treatment.

The minimum dose

A homeopathic remedy takes a lot of preparation. A tiny amount of the ingredients is diluted in water and alcohol (perhaps in the proportion 1:100), and the mixture is violently shaken. This mixture is then diluted again, and again shaken, and this can happen as many as 30 times before the medicine is ready. So the dose is extremely small – sometimes so small that there are no molecules left of the original ingredients! This process not only removes any danger from the use of poisonous ingredients, but is also believed, paradoxically, to *increase* the power of the medicine.

Is it effective?

Homeopathy is known to work well for a number of diseases, and can be used alongside conventional medical treatment. Children seem to respond well, and they like the medicines, which taste like sweets. Animals have also been treated successfully.

IDIOMS: Money

Use a dictionary to help you answer these questions.

1 Someone sold you some gold earrings *under the counter*. This means:
  a at a specially low price
  b on the black market.

2 'I'm afraid we'll all have to *tighten our belts* a bit.' This means
  a spend less money
  b work harder to make more money.

3 You're finding it difficult to *make ends meet*. This means:
  a you can't pay your debts
  b you're always short of money.

4 Which of these would you like to happen to you? Why? Why not the others?
  a to find you are *in the red*
  b to get a sudden *windfall*
  c to *pay through the nose* for something.

5 John smashed his new Porsche into a shop window. The damage came to £10,000, and his father had to *foot the bill*.
  Who paid for the damage, John or his father?

LISTENING: The limits of medicine

1 🔲 **You will hear a psychotherapist talking about the role of medicine in curing diseases. Which of these points does she make?**
  a Medical treatment often only cures people temporarily.
  b Doctors usually cure the symptoms, but not the reasons for the disease.
  c Keeping fit is a good way to stay healthy.
  d Being in touch with your inner self is a good way to stay healthy.
  e When children fall ill, it is usually the fault of their parents.
  f Migraine can usually be cured by medication.
  g A person with migraine may in fact need space for himself/herself.
  h Diseases are often a way for people to get what they want.
  i The origins of diseases can often be traced back to early childhood.
  j It isn't easy to find out what you really want in life.

2 **Here are some expressions from what the speaker says. What connection does she make between them?**
  a a knee problem – a hip problem
  b disease – fate
  c behaviour – early childhood
  d alienated – disease
  e migraine – pills
  f disease – at ease

3 **Think about what the speaker says. Do you agree with:**
  – all of it?   – not much of it?
  – most of it?   – none of it?

WORD BUILDING: Nouns and verbs (3)

1 **Nouns that are formed from verbs often have one of these endings.**

-y	-ment	-ance/-ence	-al
discovery	agreement	appearance	refusal
enquiry	argument	insistence	denial

Change the verbs in brackets into nouns. Which group do they belong to?
  a Here is an (ANNOUNCE). The (ARRIVE) of the train from Istanbul has been delayed.
  b According to the (ADVERTISE), Pizza Express has a free (DELIVER) service.
  c This is the last (REHEARSE) before the first (PERFORM) of the play.
  d Could I make an (APPOINT) to see the doctor?
  e He's been having laser (TREAT) in hospital, and he seems to be making a good (RECOVER).
  f He was a director of a large (INSURE) company, but he decided to take early (RETIRE).
  g The new headmaster has made a number of (IMPROVE) to the school.

2 **The nouns that are formed from the verbs below have unusual endings. Use a dictionary to check the correct form, then rewrite the sentences.**
  a In (COMPARE) with America, everything in Europe is on a small scale.
  b Her first novel was a great (SUCCEED), but her second was a complete (FAIL).
  c Please send any (COMPLAIN) you may have to the manager in writing.
  d I was amazed at her (KNOW) of Roman history.
  e We would like to apologise for the delayed (DEPART) of the train to Warsaw.

F Study skills: Reading between the lines

Section A: Understanding implied meaning

1 Here are the beginnings of four novels. Quickly read them (you don't have to understand every word), and decide which of them is about:

a a 19th century landowner in northern Norway who gets rid of her sick husband by faking an accident
b a young girl in an orphanage who is carried off by a giant
c the family of a wandering preacher in the USA
d a middle-aged man living alone, separated from his wife.

What helped you decide? Was it the general style or atmosphere, or did particular words or phrases give you a clue?

1
They traveled the roads and byways of the West, unhurriedly and with no set itinerary, changing their route according to the whim of the moment, the premonitory sign of a flock of birds, the lure of an unknown name. The Reeveses interrupted their erratic pilgrimage wherever they were overcome by weariness or wherever they found someone disposed to buy their intangible merchandise. They sold hope. In this way they traveled up and down the desert, they crossed mountains, and one early morning they saw day break over a beach on the Pacific coast.

2
A woman found herself at the top of a cliff in cold morning light. The sun was not shining. Around her, the mountains rose dark and watchful. The cliff was so sheer that she could not see the landscape below.

Across a wide gorge, an even steeper range of mountains stood in silent witness.

She followed every movement of the sleigh. Until it finally came to a stop against the trunk of a large birch tree at the very edge of a precipice.

The sleigh teetered slightly toward the sheer drop. Beneath were steep cliffs. And, far below, thundering rapids.

3
I am showering, breathing deeply as the steaming water, failing to numb the nerve bundle at the base of my neck, sprays a scalding reminder upon my scapulae. Hanging out flat-palmed on the turquoise tiles of my phonebooth-sized shower, I am a nobody whipped by pale fire waiting for a call. That's what I am without you, a waiting nothing, with a sore throat.

Then you called.

4
Sophie couldn't sleep.

A brilliant moonbeam was slanting through a gap in the curtains. It was shining right on to her pillow.

The other children in the dormitory had been asleep for hours.

Sophie closed her eyes and lay quite still. She tried very hard to doze off.

It was no good. The moonbeam was like a silver blade slicing through the room on to her face.

The house was absolutely silent. No voices came up from downstairs. There were no footsteps on the floor above either.

The window behind the curtain was wide open, but nobody was walking on the pavement outside. No cars went by on the street. Not the tiniest sound could be heard anywhere. Sophie had never known such a silence.

Perhaps, she told herself, this was what they called the witching hour.

2 Very often, and especially in literature, we can understand a lot from what is implied rather than stated directly.

Look at each of the texts again. Find words or phrases that imply these things:

Text 1
They are in the USA.
Mr Reeves is a wandering preacher.
He isn't very successful.
They are a superstitious family.

Text 2
It's winter.
It's a very wild, lonely place.
She isn't driving the sleigh.

Text 3
He's lonely.
He's ill
The person who phones is his wife or girlfriend.

Text 4
It's night time, probably about 4 am.
The girl lives in an orphanage.
The atmosphere is rather frightening.

Section B: Reading a poem

Stars and Planets

Trees are cages for them: water holds its breath
To balance them without smudging on its delicate meniscus.
Children watch them playing in their heavenly playground;
Men use them to lug ships across oceans, through firths.

They seem so twinkle-still, but they never cease
Inventing new spaces and huge explosions
And migrating in mathematical tribes over
The steppes of space at their outrageous ease.

It's hard to think that the earth is one –
This poor sad bearer of wars and disasters
Rolls-Roycing round the sun with its load of gangsters,
Attended only by the loveless moon.

meniscus = curved surface (of a liquid)

lug = pull (something heavy)

firth = river estuary

steppes = open grassy plains

1 [cassette] Read the poem 'Stars and Planets' by the Scottish poet Norman MacCaig. If you like, listen to the recording as you read.

2 In poetry, a single phrase often contains several implied meanings at the same time. For example, the phrase *Trees are cages for them* seems to contain these ideas:

 – If you see a star through a tree, it is framed by the branches.
 – It's as if the star is captured or held in the tree, and can't escape.
 – You can look at a star through a tree rather as you might look at an animal in a cage.

Here are some other ideas about stars and planets expressed in the first two verses of the poem. Which phrases are they expressed in?

a Sailors navigate by them.
b They move with amazing regularity over huge distances.
c They seem to move without effort.
d From looking at them, you would never guess how powerful they are.
e You can only see them reflected in absolutely still water.

3 Read the last verse of the poem. Which words seem to imply that the earth is:
 – an unhappy place?
 – a violent place?
 – a self-important place?

What contrast is the poet making between the earth and the other planets and stars?

15 Using the passive

A Active or passive?

Here are three extracts from a book called *Movie Magic*. Fill the gaps in each extract with words underneath in an appropriate form – active or passive.

A: Bloody Ending

A Western villain (1) ......*is shot*...... with the help of a special effects compressed air gun, which (2) .... soft pellets instead of bullets. The pellets (3) .... with 'blood', and (4) .... dramatically when they (5) .... their target.

burst	fire	~~shoot~~
fill	hit	

B: Make-up Ordeal

In *Frankenstein* (1933), Boris Karloff's monster make-up (1) ......*was devised*...... by Jack Pierce. The box-like head (2) .... with layers of rubber and cotton. The two metal electrodes on Karloff's neck (3) .... so tightly that he (4) .... tiny scars there for years afterwards. His face (5) .... with blue-green greasepaint, which (6) .... him the appearance of a corpse. The whole outfit (which (7) .... two huge boots) (8) .... around 22 kg. Together with the make-up, it (9) .... four hours to put on and another two to remove.

build up	fix	include
cover	give	take
~~devise~~	have	weigh

C: The Early Days

The French (1) ......*led*...... the way in turning the movies into big business, but very soon they (2) .... by the Americans. Most of the early American film-makers (3) .... on the East Coast, but there were no proper film studios. To catch the sunlight, films (4) .... on the flat roofs of tall buildings. Often, filming (5) .... by rain or smoke drifting from neighbouring chimneys. In the early 1900s these films – usually very short – (6) .... in halls all over America. These halls (7) .... 'nickelodeons' because they (8) .... a nickel (five cents) for admission.

call	charge	interrupt	~~lead~~	make	overtake	show	work

B Passive forms

Rewrite these sentences so that they use a form of the passive.

1 We understand the Minister is on his way to the airport.

The Minister ....

2 No one has ever told my fortune.

I've ....

3 She hates people staring at her.

She hates ....

4 They presented the winners with gold medals.

The winners ....

5 They're going to pierce my ears this afternoon.

I'm ....

6 We know that more than 10 per cent of the population are living in poverty.

More than 10 per cent of the population ....

7 Someone should have told us.

We ....

8 People won't obey the rules unless you enforce them.

The rules ....

9 I was sure someone was following me.

I was sure I ....

C Causes and results

Fill the gaps in the text with an appropriate form of expressions from the box.

1 This latest case of rabies is thought to have been (a) .... a bite from an infected stray dog. (b) .... widespread publicity in the international press, thousands of holiday-makers are staying away, and this has (c) .... demands from the tourist industry that all stray animals should be rounded up and destroyed.

> due to
> as a result (of)
> result (of)
> lead to
> cause
> cause of
> caused by

2 And what is the (a) .... this economic recession, which (b) .... the loss of more than 20,000 jobs in the past six weeks alone? Poor management? Poor workmanship? No. It is (c) .... one thing and one thing only: the incompetence and greed of the present government.

3 In 1979, a law was passed making it compulsory to wear seat-belts in cars. One welcome (a) .... this was a dramatic reduction in road deaths among drivers and their passengers. Unfortunately, it also (b) .... an increase in deaths among pedestrians and cyclists. Recent research suggests that drivers feel safer when they are wearing seat-belts, and (c) .... they tend to drive less carefully.

IDIOMS: Sports and games

Match the remarks on the left with the continuations on the right.

1 I think she's had rather *a raw deal*:
2 She *took* the interview *in her stride*:
3 She was very *quick off the mark*:
4 She's really *on the ball*:
5 I'm afraid she *gave the game away*:
6 She gave me a *blow-by-blow account* of the whole conversation:

a I'm quite sure they'll give her the job.
b now everyone knows we're getting engaged.
c she obviously needed to tell someone about it.
d she sold her flat the moment that prices started falling.
e she works all day and then she has to cook for everyone.
f she can tell you anything you want to know about computers.

Which of the idioms in italics do you think come originally from:

– football?   – athletics or racing?   – cards?   – boxing?

LISTENING: Oriental spices

You will hear someone talking about oriental spices and how they are used in Indian cooking. Before you begin, try to find out what these spices are called in your own language:

– cinnamon   – turmeric   – coriander
– chilli   – ginger

1 Which spices do you think are shown below?

🔲 Listen and label the pictures.

2 🔲 **Listen again and make brief notes under these headings:**

Name of spice
What it is (e.g. root, seed, leaf)
What it is like (colour, taste).

3 Which of the spices

a can be ground into a powder?
b are used to make curry powder?
c have a hot flavour?
d are mainly used for colour?
e are used in cooking rice?

COMMON VERBS: set

1 The verb *set* is mainly used in fixed expressions, and also in phrasal verbs. Look at these sentences, and match them with the paraphrases in the box.

a He decided to *set off* very early.
b The protesters *set fire to* the Embassy.
c The candle *set* the curtains *on fire*.
d Let's *set* the table for ten people.
e I'd better *set the alarm* for the morning.
f They *set to work* as soon as they arrived.
g They *set him free* after a few months.
h We watched the sun *set* over the sea.
i He *set out to* be friends with everyone.

> He was a prisoner.
> They burned it down.
> I've got to get up early.
> They started burning.
> He wanted people to like him.
> He had a long way to go.
> There was a lot to do.
> It was evening.
> We're expecting guests.

2 Here are some idiomatic expressions with *set*. What do you think they mean? Use a dictionary to help you.

a He could never get married again – he's too *set in his ways*.
b We're so disappointed – we had really *set our hearts on* buying that house.
c He was supposed to *set an example* to the others, but he behaved worse than they did.
d I won't *set foot in* their house again until they apologise to me.

16 World affairs

A From our war correspondent

Fill the gaps in these news reports. Include an item from Box A and an item from Box B in each gap, changing the form of the verb if necessary.

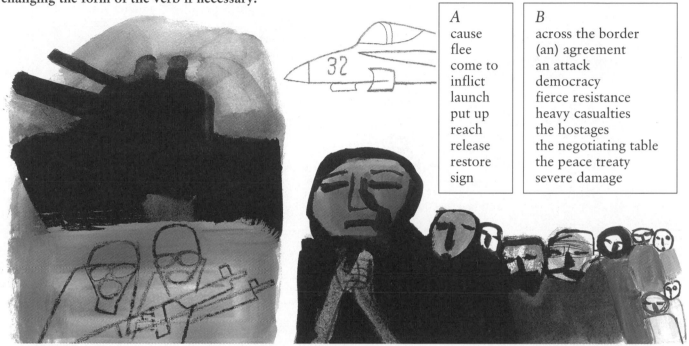

A	B
cause	across the border
flee	(an) agreement
come to	an attack
inflict	democracy
launch	fierce resistance
put up	heavy casualties
reach	the hostages
release	the negotiating table
restore	the peace treaty
sign	severe damage

1 The former President, who was removed from power by the army only three weeks after winning a general election, has promised to do all he can to .... to his country.

2 After the failure of the peace talks, rebel troops .... on the capital last night, using heavy artillery as well as tanks and mortars.

3 The Foreign Minister demanded that the terrorists should .... immediately, and said that if anyone was harmed, there would be serious consequences.

4 Millions of people around the world watched as the former enemies shook hands on the White House lawn, then sat down to ....

5 It will not be an easy victory. Troops loyal to the President .... to the invading forces, some of whom have been forced to retreat back towards the border.

6 The President claimed that Government troops .... on the rebels during the attack, and estimated the death toll to be as high as 300.

7 Yesterday's artillery attacks .... to many buildings, including the television and radio stations, the University and two hospitals.

8 Since the massacre, tens of thousands of refugees have .... in search of safety and shelter.

9 The Americans have invited representatives of both sides to .... and discuss a variety of proposals from members of the international community.

10 After months of negotiations, the two sides have finally .... about a possible end to the conflict.

B Points of view

Here are two letters to newspapers which express controversial opinions. Choose one of the opinions that you either agree or disagree with strongly, and write a few sentences explaining your own point of view.

In the past, there were good reasons for getting rid of monarchs: it is not healthy for an unelected family to hold absolute power. But these days, monarchs do not have any power: instead, they go on royal visits, support good causes, and entertain visiting heads of state – allowing the elected government more time to get on with its job. They also provide the popular press with glamorous (and sometimes scandalous) stories. Kings and queens have a useful – if very different – role in the modern world.

Dictators are out of fashion these days – everyone wants democracy instead. But does democracy work? At election time, politicians make promises, then they break them, and over the next few years, the broken promises are forgotten. And have you noticed how governments pass popular legislation only in the year before an election? Dictators may be good or they may be bad, but at least they are free to do what they think needs doing – and not spend their time worrying about opinion polls.

....
....
....
....
....
....
....

C Areas of government

All the answers are areas of government about which different political parties are likely to disagree. Read the clues and write the answers in the diagram.

1 The ....: managing the country's money (7)

2 Providing people with jobs (10)

3 Protecting the country from enemies (7)

4 Providing schools, colleges and universities (9)

5 Providing doctors, dentists, medicines, hospitals (6)

6 Providing people with somewhere to live (7)

7 Law and ....: dealing with crime (5)

8 The ....: protecting the countryside;
dealing with pollution, rubbish disposal, etc. (11)

Now use the word in the shaded squares to complete this sentence:

Politicians make promises about all of these issues at ▢▢▢▢▢▢▢▢ time.

IDIOMS: All at sea

1 Match these idioms with the pictures, which show their original meaning.

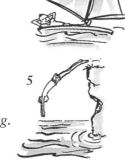

a I think you ought to *take the plunge* and tell them you're leaving home.

b I'm *in the same boat* as you – I haven't got any money saved at all.

c Their relationship has been *on the rocks* for months – and it doesn't look as if things will improve.

d The first two exam questions were really difficult, but after that it was *plain sailing*.

e Then they started talking about Einstein, and I was completely *out of my depth*.

2 Decide which of the idioms means:

a in serious trouble
b without any difficulties
c facing similar risks or problems
d unable to understand something
e take a courageous decision

LISTENING: A minimum wage?

You will hear a radio discussion about the idea of introducing a minimum wage for employees. Taking part are:

– Selina Wyatt, representing the government
– Ken Porter, representing an opposition party.

1 [cassette] Listen to the recording. What is the main reason for each speaker's attitude towards a minimum wage?

2 Which of these points do the speakers make? Write *KP*, *SW* or *N* (= neither) against each statement.

a Bosses of large companies earn far too much.
b Wages in Britain are now lower than those in Taiwan.
c If employees feel they are earning good wages, they are likely to work harder.
d If we spend too much money on wages, our companies won't be competitive.
e Large companies have plenty of money to spare.
f If company directors aren't paid enough, the best ones will leave.
g The government can't afford to help companies that go bankrupt.
h At the moment the management and the workers feel they are enemies.
i Most people think that company directors deserve the money they earn.

3 [cassette] Notice what Selina Wyatt says to agree and disagree. Listen again, and complete the sentences.

a Well, ..., where's the money going to come from?

b You're missing the point, ...

c That's a recipe for disaster, ...

WORD BUILDING: Adjectives and nouns (3)

1 Look at these examples:

Science developed rapidly in the 18th century. Newton was an important 18th century *scientist*. He made several important *scientific* discoveries.

Use a dictionary to help you complete this table.

Noun (abstract)	Noun (person)	Adjective
science	scientist	scientific
economics	....	economic
art	....	....
socialism	....	....
....	capitalist	....
....	....	optimistic
....	pessimist	....
history	historian	historical
music	....	....
politics	....	....
....	athlete	athletic
architecture	....	....
....	democrat	....

2 Correct the mistakes in these sentences.

a Don't be so pessimist. Everything will be fine.
b Who was the architectician who designed the Louvre Pyramid?
c In 1989, East Germany adopted a capitalistic system.
d She was very artistical, even as a child.
e I studied economic at university.

Answer key

Unit 1 Present, past and future

A Tenses

2	'll give	9	's doing
3	gives	10	'd left
4	've been reading	11	'm leaving / 'll be leaving
5	've read	12	left
6	was reading	13	've had
7	's doing	14	'll be having
8	will have done	15	haven't had

C Selling yourself

1 I've had/got three years' experience (of working) as a tourist guide.
2 I'm an experienced traveller.
3 I'm good at playing the piano.
   I'm a good pianist / piano player.
4 I'm a qualified English teacher / teacher of English.
5 I'm used to working long hours.

IDIOMS: Common idioms with nouns

1	a	3	b	5	a
2	b	4	b	6	b

LISTENING: Gossip

1 *a* Peter, Liz, Barbara.
   b Peter and Liz are a couple.
   c Peter is always talking on his mobile phone, wears outrageous clothes.
      Liz is very conventional.
      Barbara spends a lot of time and money making herself beautiful.
2 *a* You can't actually talk to him – you have to phone him up on his mobile phone.
   b Will you recognise him when he appears?
   c She looks like she's come out of a woman's magazine.
   d I think she has her hair done daily.
3 *a* Peter using his mobile phone during a meal.
   b Peter's tartan suit.
   c Peter and Liz.
   d Barbara (because she can afford to spend so much money at the beauty parlour).

COMMON VERBS: do and make

1 make an effort	do military service
do the washing up	do someone a favour
do your hair	make a good impression
make a mess	make an excuse
make a cup of coffee	do an exercise

2 *a* It's good enough.
   b It'll have a good effect on you.
   c I tried as hard as I could.

d I need it.
e It's not his business.
f We couldn't manage without it, we need it.
g What time is it, according to your watch?
h It would be suitable as a kitchen.
i I don't know what to think of her.
j Are you inventing it?
k I can't understand what he's saying.

Unit 2 Communicating

A Communicative phrases

1	left a message	5	sign the contract
2	made a speech	6	make an announcement
3	take notes	7	put up a notice
4	take the minutes		

C Language for talking about language

Across
2 listening 4 tense 5 noun 6 article 7 apostrophe
11 accent 13 mark 14 grammar 15 idiom
17 capital 20 future 22 verb 23 translate
25 syllable 27 preposition 29 spelling 30 past
31 simple
Down
1 personal 3 intonation 6 active 8 phrasal
9 irregular 10 person 12 comma 13 modal 16 stress
18 plural 19 adverb 21 present 24 phonology
25 superlative 26 lips 28 skills 29 stop

IDIOMS: Common idioms with prepositions

1	*a* pinch	*d* balance	*f* nutshell
	b run	*e* end	*g* glance
	c swing		
2	*a* in full swing	*e* in the long run
	b at a pinch	*f* at a loose end
	c at first glance	*g* on balance
	d in a nutshell	

LISTENING: Varieties of English

1 1 is a series of announcements at an airport. They are about flights and contacting passengers.
   2 is a telephone message on an answering machine. It is about some photos Peter has sent to a magazine.
   3 is part of a lecture, probably at a university/college/adult education centre. It is about numbers in the Finnish language.
   4 is part of the opening speech at a poetry symposium. It's about how the symposium has developed over the years.
2 *a* He's meeting someone coming from Los Angeles. She's flying to Rome.
   b Go quickly to Gate 7.

c Editor of a monthly magazine.

d In the October issue of the magazine. No – the best ones will be selected.

e Finnish and Hungarian are Finno-Ugric languages; English and Latin are Indo-European languages.

f It's the Finnish for *seven*. Unlike the numbers 1–6 in Finnish, it seems to have an Indo-European origin.

g Once a year. Ten years.

h Yes (it has 'grown from strength to strength').

i No (they haven't got a 'record number of contributions').

j Children's poetry, adult poetry, poetry written by local people: yes ('local poets of all ages'). Foreign poetry: we don't know (probably not).

WORD BUILDING: Nouns and verbs (1)

1 A exaggerate, pollute, promote
   B suggest, inject, attract
   C preserve, explain, classify
   D persuade, permit, confuse

   Words in group A change *-te* to *-tion*
   Words in group B simply add *-ion*
   Words in group C add (at least) *-ation*
   Words in D end in *-sion*

2 *a* discussion (D or B)   *e* extension (D)
   b identification (C)   *f* publication (C)
   c translation (A)   *g* explosion (D)
   d election (B)   *h* reaction (B)

Study skills A Using reference books

A Using a dictionary

1 *a* Shows how the word is pronounced.
   b Shows that it is an adjective.
   c It's an uncountable noun (we say *muzziness*, not *a muzziness*).
   d Two different definitions of the word.
   e Shows that the adverb is *muzzily*.
   f Shows where the word is divided into syllables (and where you divide it if it goes over a line).

2 *a* *myopic* (= unable to see things that are far away).
   b No; it means *a very large number*.
   c No; it means they would stop obeying you.
   d Shoot (it's a kind of gun).
   e No; it means *a fool*.
   f Both.

3 *a* mynah   *c* myrrh   *e* myelitis
   b myrtle   *d* mutinous

B Finding your way around a book

Expected answers:

1 p. 152   6 p. 29
2 p. 58, p. 75   7 p. 3
3 p. 202 (p. 221)   8 p. 275 (p. 86)
4 p. 17 (p. 228)   9 p. 174, p. 263
5 p. 231 (p. 3, p. 180)   10 p. vi

Unit 3 Making things clear

A Relative clauses

2 (that/which) I remembered from my younger days
3 which/that badly needed a coat of paint
4 who was sitting on reception
5 (that/which) he'd been writing in *or* in which he'd been writing
6 which/that said 'PRIVATE: KEEP OUT'
7 whose arms were as thick as my legs
8 (who/whom) I'd seen in the car park
9 that/which had my name on it
10 (which/that) I'd given to my daughter on her sixth birthday
11 which/that she wore day and night
12 who wants to talk to you

C Cleft sentences

1 The thing that amazes me is (the fact) that she only needs three hours' sleep a night.
2 It was in Stratford-upon-Avon that Shakespeare was born wasn't it? *or* It was Stratford-upon-Avon where …
3 What I can't stand about him is the way he smokes all the time.
4 The thing (that) I like best about France is the food.
5 It wasn't his sister (that/who) Oedipus married – it was his mother.
6 What upsets me (about them) is the fact that they never say thank you.

C Descriptive phrases

1 hidden   5 stained   8 spread
2 swinging   6 hanging (hung) 9 Lying (Sitting)
3 piled   7 coming   10 tied
4 sitting (lying)

IDIOMS: Colours

1 *c*   3 *b* *   5 *b*
2 *a*   4 *c*   6 *c*

* because if they give you a black eye, they hit you in the eye; if they give you a black look, they just look at you in an unfriendly way.

LISTENING: Radio news

1 A a legend, an Oscar, show business, a standing ovation
   B an antiques dealer, an auction, a collector's item
   C confiscate, commit suicide, offenders, complaints
   D sub-zero temperatures, fire brigade, a whimper

2 *a* true   *d* false   *g* true
   b false   *e* true   *h* false
   c false   *f* true

COMMON VERBS: get

1 a received   e answer
   b buy   f ask
   c started   g manage
   d understand   h become

2 a get down to   d get out of
   b get up to   e get on with
   c get over   f get away with

Unit 4 Sports and games

A Bungee jumping

1 a No ('it's extremely safe').
   b 50,000.
   c Yes ('all over the world').
   d No ('80% of people only ever jump once').
   e 120 metres ('from heights of up to 120 metres').
   f Terrified ('you seriously think you're going to die').
   g Relieved ('most people let out a yell of relief').
   h It makes your heart race ('up to 170 beats a minute').
   i No ('You have to be over 14').
   j Yes (if he has a medical certificate).
2 a to fall very quickly   c frightening
   b meeting   d shout

B Rules of the game

2 tackle a player   8 touches the net
3 give you a yellow card 9 change ends
4 throw the dice   10 shuffle the cards
5 collect £200   11 wins the trick
6 land on a square   12 play a trump
7 lose the point

IDIOMS: Animals

1 a donkey   c fish   e lion
   b snail   d cat   f cat
2 a a cat nap   d let the cat out of the bag
   b the lion's share   e like a fish out of water
   c at a snail's pace   f donkey work

LISTENING: Cricket

Part 1
1 He's just bowled the ball.
2 B will miss the ball and it will hit the wicket.
3 Hit the ball as far as he can. Run to the other wicket.

Part 2
1 a B will be out.
   b They will score one run.
   c B will score either four or six runs.
2 *Possible answers:*
   a … hit the wicket with the ball.
   b … in the way of the ball (so that it doesn't hit the wicket).
   c … hit the wicket with the ball.
   d …it's the other team's turn to bat.

Part 3
1 Up to five days   2 One day

WORD BUILDING: Adjectives and nouns (1)

1 A comfort, misery   D harm, use
   B industry, grammar E mud, anger
   C fame, religion
2 a space → spacious
   b adventure → adventurous
   c success → successful
   d care → careful; ice → icy
   e disaster→ disastrous
   f fashion → fashionable

Study skills B Dealing with vocabulary

B Learning new vocabulary

1 a eroded   d wailing
   b permanent   e accentuate
   c lure

Unit 5 Set in the past

B Reporting verbs

1 a denied, admitted
   b denied, admitted
   c accused
   d reminded, warned, promised
   e promised, offered, refused, (threatened)
   f threatened, (promised, offered, refused)

C Relative clauses

Possible answers:
1 … was an opium addict and a violinist as well as a brilliant detective, lived at 221B Baker Street in London, where there is now a Sherlock Holmes museum. Holmes's friend Doctor Watson, who narrates the stories, was probably based on Conan Doyle himself. The best known Sherlock Holmes story is probably *The Hound of the Baskervilles*, which Conan Doyle wrote in 1902.
2 … who was a master craftsman from Athens. Afterwards, Daedalus, whose son Icarus had come with him, was not allowed to leave. So they decided to escape using two enormous pairs of wings, which Daedalus had made out of feathers. Unfortunately Icarus, who was a typical teenager, ignored his father's warning about not flying too close to the sun. The sun melted the wax with which the feathers had been attached to the wings, and Icarus fell to his death.

IDIOMS: Numbers

1 back at the start, without making any progress
2 not sure whether to do something or not
3 very common, found everywhere
4 worked out the truth from things heard or seen
5 came as a great surprise or shock
6 at the last possible moment

Review Units 1–8

A Items 1–10

1 *b*	3 *b*	5 *d*	7 *a*	9 *c*
2 *a*	4 *d*	6 *d*	8 *b*	10 *c*

B Items 11–20

11 for	16 find/get/obtain
12 made	17 take
13 sign/accept	18 profit
14 are/get	19 experience
15 set/start	20 repairs/mends

C Items 21–32

21 denied stealing / denied (that) he had stolen
22 at a loose end
23 haven't been there for
24 The thing that annoys me
25 wasn't until I tried
26 seemed (to be) very unpleasant
27 whose husband drowned
28 they will have arrived
29 wasn't Tolstoy who/that wrote
30 they would have rung
31 nothing to do with
32 might not have received

D Items 33–42

33 they	38 ✓
34 ✓	39 the
35 to	40 had
36 me	41 ✓
37 it	42 have

E Items 43–50

43 inventor	47 illegible
44 application	48 original
45 invention	49 impractical
46 explanation	50 ridiculous

Unit 9 Possibilities

A Would it work?

1 *a* 100 seconds in a minute, 100 minutes in an hour, ten hours in a day, ten days in a week and 36 weeks in a year.
b With a five-day (or six-day) New Year holiday.
c Possible answers:
It's more logical. It's simpler. We would have the same system for time as we do for money, weights and measures. It would avoid confusion about morning and evening.
2 Possible answers:
People are used to things the way they are.
It would cost a lot to change all the clocks and watches to the new system.
People might have to work eight days a week.

People would want to have the Sabbath day every seven days, not every ten days.

B I'm not sure …

1 It depends (on) how much money I've got / whether I've got enough money / whether I can afford it.
2 It depends (on) whether I'm hungry or not / how hungry I am.
3 It depends (on) whether we can get a babysitter or not.
4 It depends on the traffic / what the traffic's like / how much traffic there is / how busy the roads are.
5 It depends (on) how busy I am / whether I'm busy or not.

C Probability

1 If you take care, you're unlikely to have any trouble.
2 Your friends are certain/sure/bound to be hungry when they arrive.
3 The thief is likely to be someone employed by the company.
4 There's certain/sure/bound to be a supermarket somewhere near here.
5 Rich people are likely to live longer than poor people.
6 There are unlikely to be too many insects at this time of year.
7 The Canadians are certain/sure/bound to do well in this year's championship.

IDIOMS: Streets and roads

1 what she is interested in or knows a lot about
2 a long way ahead
3 a situation that doesn't lead to anywhere better
4 annoying me very much
5 remote, far away from where most people are
6 very near

LISTENING: Return from Berlin

Part 1
Possible answer: The taxi driver carried her luggage onto the platform, and she waited for the train. When the train arrived, a nice little lad offered to help her with her suitcase. Then she noticed that she was surrounded by three or four strange men.
Part 2
a An inner bag with her documents and money.
b Go to the police or take the train.
c Make a statement to the police.
d Her handbag with her passport, driving licence, postcards and letters, stamps, address book, credit cards.
e Plane ticket to London, train ticket to Frankfurt, Eurocheque card.
Part 3
a … another gang of three or four men.
b … the same people she had seen before.
c … kicked them in the shinbone, 'Get out of my way! You've stolen one bag already!'
d … got off the train and disappeared.
e … a little bit better.

LISTENING: Holiday incident

1 *Part 1*
a Her (ex-)boyfriend. They were driving his Mini in Cornwall.
b An organisation that helps you if your car breaks down (= Royal Automobile Club).
Yes (they'd joined eight days earlier).
c No (she'd just passed her test).
d Slippery, and with bends in it.
Part 2
Possible answers:
a There were concrete posts at the side of the road to stop vehicles going into the river, and the car hit them.
b There was a river at the side of the road.
c The music seemed to slow down as they skidded towards the posts.
Part 3
a False (it was a 'write-off' = too badly damaged to drive).
b False (they watched unsympathetically).
c True (13 hours).
d False (they were covered by their insurance).
e True (their neighbours were 'disgusted').
2 *a* who was my boyfriend at the time
which is a very small car
which helps you if you break down
which seemed to be overtaking at the time
b Luckily we'd joined the RAC eight days earlier
I'd just passed my test
I hadn't had really a lot of experience

COMMON VERBS: go

1 *a* It's disappeared.
b It leads there.
c It's how she spends it.
d Start running.
e It's the noise it made.
f It's not fresh.
g Put it there.
h There's no room for it.
i It won't start.
j I can't speak.
k It was a success.
l I can't remember it.
2 *a* lost all its money
b he never stops (working)
c be spontaneous (don't worry how you behave)
d looks good with
e the price has increased

Unit 6 Do it yourself

A Getting the picture

1 Inserting batteries: K, M
Loading the camera: N, G, E, O
Taking a photo: A, I (or I, A), C, J, L
Rewinding the film: H, D, F, B

2 *a* an extended period
b insufficient
c ensure
d insert
e displays
f positioned correctly
g obscured
h remove

B Things need doing

1 stain; missing; sewing
2 redecorating; peeling; cracks
3 damp; leak; repaired
4 rotten; replaced

C Verbs in the kitchen

1 simmer	5 peel	8 chop
2 bake	6 sprinkle	9 serve
3 stir	7 slice	10 fry
4 melt		

In the shaded squares: Master chef

IDIOMS: Parts of the body (1)

1 *a* head   *d* eyes   *f* fingers
b brain   *e* leg   *g* head
c head, heels
2 *a* up to my eyes in
b have got … on the brain
c over my head
d cross my fingers (for you)
e off the top of my head
f head over heels
g pull someone's leg

LISTENING: How to do it

1 A brush, stir, drip, can
B finger, thumb, hole, blow (stick)
C hole, sandpaper, stick, finger, glue
2 A Stir, mixed. Press, brush, can, dripping. Brush, brush.
B Hold. Cover, hole, thumb, finger, hole, blow.
C Rub, hole, sandpaper, glue, finger. Peel, press, hole, dry.

WORD BUILDING: Prefixes (1)

2 uncomfortable   unfortunate
illegible   impractical
inedible   illiterate
unexpected   inaudible
impatient   irrelevant
3 *a* inedible   *d* irrelevant
b inaudible   *e* illegible
c illiterate   *f* unfortunate

Study skills C Approaching a reading text

B Reading for the main idea

2 *a* Minor detail   *e* Main point
b Main point   *f* Main point
c Main point   *g* Minor detail
d Minor detail

C Finding specific information

Possible answers:

1 *Datura arborea* (common name: borrachero)
   – small tree with large bell-shaped flowers
   – fruit contains dangerous drug scopolamine

   Grows wild in Colombia and other South American countries.

   Grown in Ecuador to produce drugs for pharmaceutical industry.

2 Burundanga (popular name for scopolamine)
   Used by criminals, mainly for robbery, also rape.

   Effect: 'hypnosis', causes victims to lose memory and do whatever they are told. No memory afterwards of what happened.

   Appearance: white or yellow powder, soluble, odourless and tasteless.

   Is given to victims in food or drink (e.g. sweets, chocolate, spirits, cola drinks).

Unit 7 Working it out

A Taking sides

Possible answers:

1 The Earth can't be flat. Otherwise people would keep falling off the edge
2 The Vikings can't have discovered America. If they had, Americans would all speak Norwegian.
3 The sun can't be cooling down. If it was/were, the Earth would be getting cooler.
4 Father Christmas must exist. Otherwise the children wouldn't get their presents.
5 There can't be a monster in Loch Ness. If there was/were, there'd be some scientific evidence for it.
6 Lord Lucan must have committed suicide. Otherwise he would have been found by now.

B Appearance and the senses

1 They seem to be enjoying themselves.
2 You sound as if / as though you have a cold.
3 They appear to have left the country.
4 Those roses smell beautiful.
5 She looks like her mother.
6 They seem (to be) very pleasant.

IDIOMS: Parts of the body (2)

1 I landed on my feet
2 she put a brave face on it
3 He's set his heart on becoming an airline pilot
4 Could you lend me a hand?
5 we see eye to eye
6 I was racking my brains

LISTENING: Life elsewhere?

2 *a* three   *b* one
3 *a* 3   *c* 1   *e* 1, 2   *g* 2
   b 4   *d* –   *f* 4

COMMON VERBS: come

1 *a* That's how deep it was.   *g* She can't accept it.
   b That's what I decided.   *h* We could see it.
   c It's more important.   *i* I could use them.
   d That's its position.   *j* People are wearing it.
   e It happened slowly.   *k* She was the winner.
   f That's its origin.   *l* That's the total.
2 *a* found (by chance)   *d* were convinced by
   b find   *e* it's simply a question of
   c visit me (casually)

Unit 8 In the market-place

B Business verbs

1 rose; made a profit; take on
2 make a loss; lay off
3 took out; pay off
4 was made redundant; set up
5 break even

IDIOMS: Describing feelings

1 *a* terrified   *d* unable to decide
   b very happy   *e* angry
   c desperate   *f* nervous
2 *a* scared stiff   *d* on edge
   b at his wits' end   *e* on top of the world
   c up in arms about it   *f* completely at a loss

LISTENING: The new design manager

1 *a* Nick and Lisa
   b *Possible answers:*
      Sandra: someone from outside, has experience as a manager
      Nick: has experience, reliability
      Lisa: very talented, has initiative
2 happiest as part of a team: L –
   reliable and stable: N +
   lots of creative flair: L +
   has no direct design experience: S –
   has been with the company for one year: L –
   three years as a project manager: S +
   combines stability and creativity: S +
3 *Possible answers:*
   Lisa or Nick: not yet at management level, they work well together as part of a team
   Sandra: it might cause bad feeling among the staff (because she's coming in from outside)
4 Probably Sandra. The boss (who's chairing the meeting) hints that she favours her.

WORD BUILDING: Nouns and verbs (2)

1 investigate, investigation   employer, employment
   operate, operator   survive, survivor
   translator, translation   apply, application
   invest, investor   rob, robbery
2 *a* competition   *d* applicants
   b investigation   *e* survivors
   c invested

COMMON VERBS: see

1 *a* find out   *e* be sure
   b understand   *f* finds attractive
   c consider (it)   *g* speak to
   d imagine   *h* accompany
2 *a* It's getting old, it's no longer in good condition.
   b I've been spending a lot of time with him.
   c I was imagining something that wasn't there.
   d We ought to make arrangements to hire a car.
   e I'll be glad when he goes away.
   f Come to the station with me to say goodbye.
   g It was clear to everybody that it wasn't true.

Unit 10 Life, the universe and everything

A Five scientists

1 G astronomer, planets, revolves
   D evolved, mutations, species
   C element, radiation, uranium ore
   E atomic bombs, energy, time
   W earthquakes, fault lines, mountains
2 *a* False ('hearing about the invention …').
   b True.
   c False (he said, 'Yet it moves').
   d False ('Others are beneficial').
   e True.
   f True.
   g True ('Time will pass more slowly for someone travelling in space').
   h False.
   i True.
   j False. They're still drifting.

B Environmental issues

Possible answers:

The greenhouse effect is caused by burning fossil fuels like oil and coal. These fuels give off greenhouse gases, which trap heat in the earth's atmosphere, and lead to global warming.

The ozone layer protects us from the ultra-violet light which comes from the sun. There is now a hole in the ozone layer, which was caused by chemicals like CFCs, which are used in fridges. Because of this, more people are getting skin cancer.

Nuclear power stations produce radioactive waste which remains dangerous for a very long time. Since we can't get rid of this waste, it will have to be stored in special containers, perhaps for thousands of years.

As human beings use up more and more of the earth for cities and agriculture, we are destroying the natural habitats of many plants and animals. Because of this, many species are becoming extinct every year.

IDIOMS: Things people say

1 *a*   3 *b*   5 *a*
2 *b*   4 *a*   6 *b*

LISTENING: Reading the tarot

2 Card A represents a balance between opposites; new knowledge; peace and harmony.
   Up to now, there have been *conflicts/contradictions* in the person's life. Now she is starting to *resolve them* and to find *a new way forward*.
3 Card B represents the feminine principle; creativity and rebirth; a new beginning.
   There's going to be a *fundamental change* in the person's life. She's going to break free from *old habits* and go through a period of *intense feelings*.
4 *a* Yes (a new beginning, life taking a new direction).
   b No.
   c Yes (a new job, creativity, a period of excitement).

WORD BUILDING: Adjectives and nouns (2)

1 possible, safe; patient, important; long, deep; dark, lazy; urgent, pregnant
2 *a* generosity, intelligence, self-confidence
   b strength, *fitness*
   c complexity
   d humidity, fertility
   e efficiency, punctuality
   f *laziness*, stupidity

Study skills D Summarising information

A Taking notes

1 Set B shows how the information is *organised* (how it is divided up, what are the main points, how many different points). Set A just lists all the points equally, without showing the connections between them.

   Possible answers for points 3 and 4:
   3. green spaces for people to use
   4. habitat for plants and animals (grass, trees, ponds, etc.)

2 *Possible answers:*
   Looking after green roofs
   Depends on type of green roof:
   1. 'extensive' green roof
      – thin layer of of soil, mostly grass
      – doesn't need looking after
   2. trees and shrubs
      – need more soil
      – need looking after (like a garden)
   Possible problems
   1. Technical
      – roof can start leaking
      – roots of plants can destroy roof
      Nowadays, technology to solve problems (damp courses, root protection systems)
   2. Cost
      People think green roofs cost more.
      But no longer true: green roofs cost the same per square metre as tiled roofs.

B Writing a summary

1 – A small amount of factual information added to 'fill out' the sentences: *people were suspicious of green roofs; technology is more developed now.*
– Sentences are joined: *because, and, as, also.*
– Information is made clearer: *have several advantages; the most important …; rainwater that would otherwise be wasted.*

Possible sentences to cover points 3 and 4:
They also provide green spaces for people to use in densely crowded cities, and an important habitat for plants and animals.

2 *Possible summary:*
How much green roofs need looking after depends on the type. Green roofs which consist mostly of grass do not need looking after at all. Green roofs that have trees and shrubs need to be looked after in the same way as a normal garden.

Some people are worried about technical problems connected with green roofs, for example that the roof could leak or that roots could destroy it. But nowadays technology has been developed and these problems have been resolved. Also, green roofs are no longer expensive; in fact they cost the same per square metre as tiled roofs.

Unit 11 Evaluating

A Then and now

Possible answers:
1 There are a lot more cars than there used to be.
2 People used to go to the cinema a lot more often than they do now.
3 Trains used to be much more frequent than they are now.
4 Classes are much smaller than they used to be.
5 We eat meat far more often than we used to.

C Good and bad effects

Possible answers:
1 The scheme will enable people to do all their shopping at the same time.
2 It'll prevent people from driving to work.
3 It'll discourage people from shopping in the town centre.
4 It'll save people from sitting in rush-hour queues.
5 It'll encourage people to use buses and trains.
6 It'll force people to drive for miles to do their shopping.
7 It'll make it easier for pedestrians to get around the centre.

IDIOMS: Other people

1 *a*
2 *b*

3 Only Diana. If someone *gets your back up*, you find them annoying. If someone *gives you the creeps*, you find it very unpleasant to be anywhere near them. Someone *on the same wavelength* as you thinks the same way as you do.
4 *c*

LISTENING: Panel discussion

1 It's something everyone should do.   *no one*
In general, it's worthwhile.   C
In general, it isn't worth it.   A
There's absolutely no point in it.   B
2 *a* B   *d* A   *f* A
  b A   *e* –   *g* C
  c B
3 *Possible answers:*
  a how much of the money disappears into the pockets of dishonest people
  b people who want to do good (but in fact don't)
  c honestly meaning to help
  d interfering with the natural flow of rivers etc.

COMMON VERBS: take

1 *a* They captured them.   *g* I didn't like her.
  b I started doing it.   *h* It's missing.
  c I wasn't concentrating.   *i* I'm like her.
  d I didn't mean it.   *j* You can use either.
  e It was a long journey.   *k* I wrote them down.
  f Swallow them.

2 *a* feel hurt or upset
  b sees it as important
  c I wasn't expecting it
  d assumed it (without questioning)
  e participating in (running in the race)
  f do it as slowly as you like

Unit 12 Yourself and others

A Personality adjectives

1 positive, optimistic, cheerful
2 inquisitive, nosy
3 thoughtful, reflective
4 selfish, vain
5 communicative, sociable
6 insecure, shy, timid
7 aggressive
8 oversensitive
9 easy-going, placid, calm, amenable
10 fussy

B Laura's dream

1 *According to the book's interpretation:*
   a her feelings about the wedding; the heavy shoes
   b the black colours of her clothes and the flowers
   c her veil
   d the 'explosion' of the bouquet
   e the dead, black roses
   f the butterfly
   g the potatoes
   h the unsympathetic crowd
   i she couldn't pick up the rubbish
   j the aisle sloping downwards
   k the crowd poking her and telling her to clear up the mess
   l the bright colours of the butterfly
2 According to the book: 'While the dream was clearly summing up her present situation and her deep depression and reluctance, there was also a message of hope.'

IDIOMS: Reactions

1 He decided to turn a blind eye (to it).
2 You shouldn't take it to heart.
3 She decided that the time had come for her to speak her mind.
4 At the last minute, they got cold feet.
5 It's time you put your foot down.
6 It goes against the grain for me to complain about things.

LISTENING: Two jokes

1 *See tapescript*
2 *Possible answers:*
   Joke A: cruelty, domination of women, control over other people
   Joke B: control over other people, materialistic attitudes, meanness

WORD BUILDING: Prefixes (2)

1 *mis-*   in the wrong way
  dis-   not, the opposite of
  over-   too much
  under- not enough
  re-   again, back
2 a overslept   e rewrite
  b misbehave   f misinterpreted
  c dissatisfied   g underprivileged
  d disapproves

3 a someone with poor judgment, mistaken beliefs
  b to lose a baby while you are pregnant
  c to be disappointed in something you once believed in
  d to think that something is bigger or better than it really is
  e saying that something is smaller or less important than it really is

Unit 13 Right and wrong

A They were all to blame

Possible answers:
1 The boy shouldn't have been playing in the street; he shouldn't have run out into the road; he should have looked before he ran out into the road.
2 The driver shouldn't have been driving so fast; he should have been looking where he was going.
3 The authorities should have put a sign up; they should have provided a safe play area for children.
4 The boy's parents shouldn't have let their son play in the street.
5 The Tylers shouldn't have been making a noise so late; they should have turned the sound down when they were asked; they should have used headphones.
6 Mr Kent shouldn't have burst into the house; he shouldn't have smashed the Tylers' equipment; he should have waited for the police to arrive.
7 The police should have got there more quickly.

B Could, should, needn't and might

2 I needn't have made all those sandwiches.
3 I could (easily) have met you at the station.
4 You might/could have told me you were eating out!
5 He needn't have been so rude.
6 She should have been sent to prison.
7 You could/might have been recognised.

IDIOMS: All in the mind

1 a   3 b   5 b
2 a   4 b   6 a

LISTENING: Mistakes

2 *Story A*
   a He tried to get in through the door.
   b She slammed the door.
   c It was jammed in the door.
   d She thought he just wanted to get into the party.
   e Because he was really hurt, and he was in tears.
   f She put a tea-towel round his thumb.
   g It was in a plaster, and was sticking up as if he was hitch-hiking.
   h Because she never confessed that she had done it (he didn't know who had slammed the door).

Story B

a Because he was tired ('knackered') the night before.
b He left it in an envelope pinned to the door.
c In the basement, with a separate entrance.
d That they'd been burgled.
e He/She had taken the key and opened the door.
f The speaker's video and other things.

COMMON VERBS: put

2 *a* put up with
  b put things off
  c put you up
  d put it down to
  e put me down
  f puts you off
  g put across
  h put it down

Unit 14 Body and mind

A Talking about diseases

1	symptom	9	research
2	disease	10	infected
3	developed	11	diarrhoea
4	injection	12	contact
5	vaccinate	13	immune
6	parasite	14	fever
7	repellent	15	pregnant
8	antibiotics	16	treated

The circled letters spell *medical treatment*.

B The man who was dead

surgery; patient; temperature; examination; x-ray; prescription; appointment; psychiatrist; bleed; Blood; bleed.

C Homeopathy

1 *a* Fairly recent – less than 200 years.
  b No – they're heavily diluted.
  c Yes.
  d *Not answered in the text.*
  e Yes.
  f *Not answered in the text.*
2 *a* the medicine that most people use
  b *flushed* = red coloured
    hallucinations = seeing things that aren't there
  c indigestion, diarrhoea
  d medicine
  e the amount of medicine a person takes
  f If something is *paradoxical*, it seems to contradict itself: if the medicine has less in it, you would expect it to be weaker, but in fact it is stronger.

IDIOMS: Money

1 *b*   2 *a*   3 *b*
4 *a* No – it means you're in debt.
  b Yes – it means getting money you weren't expecting.
  c No – it means it costs a lot of money.
5 John's father.

LISTENING: The limits of medicine

1 *a, b, d, g, h, i, j*
2 *a* A person may cure a knee problem, and then have a hip problem later on, with the same cause.
  b Disease is not caused by fate.
  c People's behaviour is learned in early childhood.
  d If a person feels alienated from himself/herself, they are more likely to get a disease.
  e Migraine cannot be cured by pills.
  f The word *disease* means 'not at ease'.

WORD BUILDING: Nouns and verbs (3)

1 *a* announcement, arrival
  b advertisement, delivery
  c rehearsal, performance
  d appointment
  e treatment, recovery
  f insurance, retirement
  g improvements
2 *a* comparison
  b success, failure
  c complaints
  d knowledge
  e departure

Study skills F Reading between the lines

A Understanding implied meaning

1 *a* 2   *b* 4   *c* 1   *d* 3
2 *Text 1*
  They are in the USA: *the West*; *the Pacific coast*.
  Mr Reeves is a wandering preacher: *traveled the roads and byways*; *they sold hope*
  He isn't very successful: *wherever they found someone disposed to buy their intangible merchandise*
  They are a superstitious family: *the premonitory sign of a flock of birds*

  Text 2
  It's winter: *cold morning light*; *the sleigh*
  It's a very wild, lonely place: *the mountains rose dark and watchful*; *stood in silent witness*; *far below, thundering rapids*
  The woman isn't driving the sleigh: *she followed every movement of the sleigh* (she was watching it from a distance)

  Text 3
  He's lonely: *I am a nobody*; *waiting for a call*; *a waiting nothing*
  He's ill: *failing to numb the nerve bundle*; *with a sore throat*
  The person who phones is his wife or girlfriend: *that's what I am without you*

  Text 4
  It's night time, probably about 4 am: *a brilliant moonbeam*; *the other children had been asleep for hours*; *nobody was walking on the pavement*; *no cars went by on the street*
  The girl lives in an orphanage: *the other children in the dormitory*
  The atmosphere is rather frightening: *had never known such a silence*; *this was what they called the witching hour*

B Reading a poem

Possible answers:

2 *a* Men use them to lug ships across oceans
   b migrating in mathematical tribes over / The steppes
      of space
   c at their outrageous ease
   d They seem so twinkle-still
   e water holds its breath / To balance them without
      smudging on its delicate meniscus

3 unhappy: *sad bearer, wars, disasters, loveless moon*
   violent: *wars, gangsters*
   self-important: *Rolls-Roycing* (= going round like a
   Rolls Royce)
   Contrast: The stars and planets look delicate and
   harmless but are in fact magnificent and powerful; we
   believe the Earth is the centre of everything but in fact
   it is small and lonely.

Unit 15 Using the passive

A Active or passive?

A: *Bloody Ending*

2	fires	4	burst
3	are filled	5	hit

B: *Make-up Ordeal*

2	was built up	6	gave
3	were fixed	7	included
4	had	8	weighed
5	was covered	9	took

C: *The Early Days*

2	were overtaken	6	were shown
3	worked	7	were called
4	were made	8	charged
5	was interrupted		

B Passive forms

1 The Minister is understood to be on his way to the
   airport.
2 I've never had my fortune told.
3 She hates being stared at.
4 The winners were presented with gold medals.
5 I'm going to have my ears pierced this afternoon.
6 More than 10 per cent of the population are known to
   be living in poverty.
7 We should have been told.
8 The rules won't be obeyed unless they're enforced.
9 I was sure I was being followed.

C Causes and results

1 *a* caused by, the result of, due to
   b As a result of, Due to
   c led to
2 *a* cause of
   b has led to, has caused
   c due to, the result of, caused by
3 *a* result of   *b* led to   *c* as a result

IDIOMS: Sports and games

1	*e*	3	*d*	5	*b*
2	*a*	4	*f*	6	*c*

Possible answers:
Football: on the ball
Athletics/racing: quick off the mark; in her stride
Cards: a raw deal; gave the game away
Boxing: blow-by-blow

LISTENING: Oriental spices

1 *a* chilli   *c* cinnamon   *e* turmeric
   b coriander   *d* ginger
2 *Possible answers:*
   Ginger. Root of a plant. Very hot, peppery. Brown.
   Chilli. Fruit of a plant. Mild or very hot. Red.
   Turmeric. Root of a plant. Made into powder. Rich,
   woody. Yellow.
   Coriander. Seeds (leaves also used). Warm, rich
   flavour. Brown.
   Cinnamon. Bark of a tree. Aromatic. Brown.
3 *a* all of them
   b chilli, turmeric, coriander
   c ginger, chilli
   d turmeric
   e turmeric, cinnamon

COMMON VERBS: set

1 *a* He had a long way to go.
   b They burned it down.
   c They started burning.
   d We're expecting guests.
   e I've got to get up early.
   f There was a lot to do.
   g He was a prisoner.
   h It was evening.
   i He wanted people to like him.
2 *a* He has fixed habits.
   b We wanted it very much.
   c He was supposed to show others how to behave
      well.
   d I won't enter their house again.

Unit 16 World affairs

A From our war correspondent

1 restore democracy
2 launched an attack
3 release the/their hostages
4 sign the peace treaty
5 are putting up / have put up / have been putting up
   fierce resistance
6 had inflicted heavy casualties
7 caused severe damage
8 fled across the border
9 come to the negotiating table
10 reached (an) agreement
    come to an agreement

C Areas of government

1 economy   5 health
2 employment   6 housing
3 defence   7 order
4 education   8 environment
In the shaded squares: election

IDIOMS: All at sea

1 *a* 5   *c* 2   *e* 3
   b 1   *d* 4
2 *a* on the rocks
   b plain sailing
   c in the same boat
   d out of my depth
   e take the plunge

LISTENING: A minimum wage?

1 *Suggested answer:*
Ken Porter wants a minimum wage for employees.
Selina Wyatt wants to allow companies to pay what
they can afford.
2 *a* KP   *d* SW   *g* N
   b N   *e* KP   *h* KP
   c KP   *f* SW   *i* N
3 *a* as you say
   b if you don't mind my saying
   c if you ask me

WORD BUILDING: Adjectives and nouns (3)

1 economist
   artist, artistic
   socialist, socialist
   capitalism, capitalist
   optimism, optimist
   pessimism, pessimistic
   musician, musical
   politician, political
   athletics
   architect, architectural
   democracy, democratic
2 *a* pessimistic   *d* artistic
   b architect   *e* economics
   c capitalist

Review Units 9–16

A Items 1–10

1 *c*   4 *c*   7 *c*   9 *b*
2 *a*   5 *c*   8 *a*   10 *d*
3 *a*   6 *d*

B Items 11–20

11 disease   16 research
12 rest/others   17 might/could/would
13 against   18 which
14 case   19 destroyed
15 done   20 case

C Items 21–32

21 is unlikely to
22 reached agreement / reached an agreement / came to
    an agreement
23 needn't have brought
24 make it easier (for us)
25 is reported to be
26 led to / resulted in / caused the loss of
27 (well) worth visiting / (well) worth a visit
28 having his photograph taken
29 my blood boil
30 than we do now
31 take offence
32 prevented the burglars from leaving

D Items 33–42

33 were   38 do
34 more   39 any
35 ✓   40 up
36 it   41 ✓
37 ✓   42 ✓

E Items 43–50

43 argument   47 awareness
44 political   48 economist
45 tendency   49 depth
46 dishonest   50 democratic

Irregular verbs

Infinitive	Simple past	Past participle
be	was/were	been
beat	beat	beaten
become	became	become
begin	began	begun
bend	bent	bent
bite	bit	bitten
blow	blew	blown
break	broke	broken
bring	brought	brought
burn	burnt	burnt
build	built	built
buy	bought	bought
can	could	(been able)
catch	caught	caught
choose	chose	chosen
come	came	come
cost	cost	cost
cut	cut	cut
do	did	done
draw	drew	drawn
dream	dreamt	dreamt
drink	drank	drunk
drive	drove	driven
eat	ate	eaten
fall	fell	fallen
feed	fed	fed
feel	felt	felt
fight	fought	fought
find	found	found
fly	flew	flown
forget	forgot	forgotten
forgive	forgave	forgiven
freeze	froze	frozen
get	got	got
give	gave	given
go	went	gone (been)
grow	grew	grown
hang	hung	hung
have	had	had
hear	heard	heard
hide	hid	hidden
hit	hit	hit
hold	held	held
hurt	hurt	hurt
keep	kept	kept
know	knew	known
lay	laid	laid
lead	led	led
learn	learnt	learnt
leave	left	left
lend	lent	lent
let	let	let
lie	lay	lain
lose	lost	lost
make	made	made
mean	meant	meant
meet	met	met
pay	paid	paid
put	put	put
read	read	read
ride	rode	ridden
ring	rang	rung
rise	rose	risen
run	ran	run
say	said	said
see	saw	seen
sell	sold	sold
send	sent	sent
set	set	set
shake	shook	shaken
shine	shone	shone
shoot	shot	shot
show	showed	shown
shut	shut	shut
sing	sang	sung
sink	sank	sunk
sit	sat	sat
sleep	slept	slept
smell	smelt	smelt
speak	spoke	spoken
spell	spelt	spelt
spend	spent	spent
spread	spread	spread
stand	stood	stood
steal	stole	stolen
sweep	swept	swept
swim	swam	swum
swing	swung	swung
take	took	taken
teach	taught	taught
tear	tore	torn
tell	told	told
think	thought	thought
throw	threw	thrown
understand	understood	understood
wake	woke	woken
wear	wore	worn
win	won	won
write	wrote	written

Phonetic symbols

Vowels

Symbol	Example
/iː/	tree /triː/
/i/	many /'meni/
/ɪ/	sit /sɪt/
/e/	bed /bed/
/æ/	back /bæk/
/ʌ/	sun /sʌn/
/ɑː/	car /kɑː/
/ɒ/	hot /hɒt/
/ɔː/	horse /hɔːs/
/ʊ/	full /fʊl/
/uː/	moon /muːn/
/ɜː/	girl /gɜːl/
/ə/	arrive /ə'raɪv/
	water /'wɔːtə/
/eɪ/	late /leɪt/
/aɪ/	time /taɪm/
/ɔɪ/	boy /bɔɪ/
/əʊ/	home /həʊm/
/aʊ/	out /aʊt/
/ɪə/	hear /hɪə/
/eə/	there /ðeə/
/ʊə/	pure /pjʊə/

Consonants

Symbol	Example
/p/	pull /pʊl/
/b/	bad /bæd/
/t/	take /teɪk/
/d/	dog /dɒg/
/k/	cat /kæt/
/g/	go /gəʊ/
/tʃ/	church /tʃɜːtʃ/
/dʒ/	age /eɪdʒ/
/f/	for /fɔː/
/v/	love /lʌv/
/θ/	thick /θɪk/
/ð/	this /ðɪs/
/s/	sit /sɪt/
/z/	zoo /zuː/
/ʃ/	shop /ʃɒp/
/ʒ/	leisure /'leʒə/
/h/	house /haʊs/
/m/	make /meɪk/
/n/	name /neɪm/
/ŋ/	bring /brɪŋ/
/l/	look /lʊk/
/r/	road /rəʊd/
/j/	young /jʌŋ/
/w/	wear /weə/

Stress

We show stress by a mark (/'/) before the stressed syllable:
later /'leɪtə/; arrive /ə'raɪv/; information /ɪnfə'meɪʃn/.

Acknowledgements

The authors and publishers are grateful to the following copyright owners for permission to reproduce copyright material. Every endeavour has been made to contact copyright owners and apologies are expressed for any omissions.

Addison Wesley Longman Ltd for the extract on p. 16 from the *Longman Dictionary of Contemporary English* (*3rd edition*); Penguin Books for the contents page on p. 17 from the *Time Out Guide to Prague*; Wiltshire Sport and Leisure for the article on p. 21; Ewan MacNaughton Associates for the texts on p. 22 and p. 75-76 from the Daily Telegraph; Sheila Land Associates Ltd for the extract on p. 25 from *In search of Genghis Khan* by Tim Severin, published by Arrow Books; Le Monde for the article on pp. 32 & 33; Dorling Kindersley for the texts on pp. 54 & 74 from *The Complete Book of Dreams* by Julia and Derek Parker; Gyldendal Norsk Forlag for text 1 on p. 64, © Gyldendal Norsk Forlag A/S 1989, taken from *Dina's Book* by Herbjorg Wassmo, published by Corgi, an imprint of Transworld Publishers Ltd. All rights reserved; HarperCollins Publishers for text 2 on p. 64 from *The Infinite Plan* by Isabel Allende, © HarperCollins 1994; Fourth Estate Ltd for text 3 on p. 64 from *Troutstream* by Gerald Lynch, © 1995 Gerald Lynch. Reproduced with permission from Fourth Estate Ltd; David Higham Associates Ltd for text 4 on p. 64 from *The BFG* by Roald Dahl, published by Jonathan Cape; The Estate of Norman MacCaig for the poem on p. 65 from Collected Poems, published by Chatto & Windus; S W Books for the pictures on p. 66, © S W Books, 5-11 Mortimer Street, London W1N 7RH; Wayland Publisher for the text on p. 66 from *Movie Magic* by Robin Cross.

The authors and publishers are grateful to the following illustrators, photographers and photographic sources:

Illustrators: Richard Deverell: p. 23; Hilary Evans: handwriting on pp. 24, 33, 48, 49, 56; Gecko Limited: all DTP illustrations and graphics; Phil Healey: p. 34; Amanda MacPhail: pp. 37, 71; Michael Ogden: pp. 30, 47; Pantelis Palios: p. 12; Martin Sanders: p. 45; Kath Walker: p. 35; Dan Williams: p. 18, 42; Rosemary Woods: p. 65; Annabel Wright: pp. 54, 69.

Photographic sources: Heather Angel/Biophotos: p. 32; The J. Allan Cash Photolibrary: p. 57 *t*; Mary Evans Picture Library: p. 27; Peter Kanab: p. 68; B. Moser/The Hutchison Library: p. 25; Pictor International: p. 57 *b*; Roland Stifter: p. 48 (taken from *Roof Gardens, Green Isles in the Cities*); Wiltshire Sport and Leisure: p. 21.

t = top   *b* = bottom

Picture research by Sandie Huskinson-Rolfe of PHOTOSEEKERS.

Cover design by Dunne & Scully.

Design, production and repro handled by Gecko Limited, Bicester, Oxon.

Permissions cleared by Sophie Dukan.

Sound recordings by Martin Williamson, Prolingua Productions at Studio AVP.

Freelance editorial work by Meredith Levy.